The (Spiri
of (

The (Spiritual) @dventures of CyberCindy

Gill Rowell

PATERNOSTER PRESS

Copyright 2003 Gill Rowell

First published in 2003 by Paternoster Press

09 08 07 06 05 04 03   7 6 5 4 3 2 1

Paternoster Press is an imprint of Authentic Media,
P.O. Box 300, Carlisle, Cumbria, CA3 0QS, UK
and
P.O. Box 1047, Waynesboro, GA 30830-2047, USA

Website: www.paternoster-publishing.com

British Library Cataloguing in Publication Data
A catalogue record for this book is available from the British Library

ISBN 1-84227-170-9

Cover Design by FourNineZero
Typeset by WestKey Ltd, Falmouth, Cornwall
Printed in Great Britain by Cox & Wyman, Reading, Berkshire

'An interesting and unusual analogy of biblical truth, told in a 21st-century way for those more familiar with the internet than the illustrated pages of a book!'
— Fiona Castle —

'*CyberCindy* is the most exciting, un-put-downable Christian book I have ever read ... Buy it quick.'
— John Goldingay —

'This is an exciting and exhilarating little gem. With one hand taking a firm grasp of important and familiar biblical narratives and the other hand reaching into the minds of young, switched on, twenty-first century thinkers, Gill Rowell has made an electrifying connection that will equip her readers to interpret and apply God's changeless Word in a constantly changing world.'
— Paul H Brooks, Director NOVI MOST International —

'An exciting read! CyberCindy's interactive exasperations at times echoing our struggles for easy answers.'
— Jacky Russell, Housewife, Artist and 'ordinary' Christian —

'... the book will be of tremendous interest to young people, making an impact upon them and giving an entirely new aspect to the Bible which I hope young people will understand.'
— Ron Egner, Vice-President of British Youth for Christ —

'It is rare to read an entirely original book. But this is one. Gill displays wonderfully imaginative and creative skills to teach some very challenging parts of the Bible. She does so without sacrificing depth or quality. A rare combination. I hope it is widely read.'
— Derek Tidball, Principal of London Bible College —

'*The (Spiritual) @dventures of CyberCindy* leads us on an illuminating hi-tech journey back to the Old Testament book of Ruth. A fascinating and erudite dialogue between Christian thought and 21st-century scepticism, it reads like a spiritual retake on *Alice in Wonderland*, full of ideas and provocation.'
— Stuart Broom, Waterstone's Booksellers, Nottingham —

'As a young and passionate teenager, I prayed that God would allow me to travel back as an unseen follower of Jesus – wishing only to observe and not interfere. *The (Spiritual) @dventures of CyberCindy* almost makes the "not yet" now. In what could easily be mistaken for a proposal for a real-to-life virtual project, you actually get a sense of what it may have been like to be Ruth's travel companion. Travelling with (or as) CyberCindy allows you to raise questions of your own as well as those provoked during the Adventures.'
— Gorton Brown, Interactive E-Learning Developer, BBC —

For Jenny

Contents

Acknowledgements

I would like to record my thanks and appreciation to my husband, James, for his encouragement, love and care for me in all my endeavours; to my daughters, Phoebe and Rachael, for their excited approval and their willingness to do those things I would be doing if I wasn't writing or reading; to my friends Mandy and Sarah, who shared ideas with me as CyberCindy was being created. I would also particularly like to thank Mary Evans for her crucial encouragement, Conrad Gempf for his enthusiasm and Nick Mercer for his inspiration, all those days ago, when I was a student at London Bible College. I would also like to thank Paul Brooks for his theological acumen and for giving me a creative environment from which to flourish.

Foreword

Just occasionally a book emerges which completely defies classification. Written on a variety of levels it can equally well be read on different levels bringing stimulation, challenge and enjoyment to virtually any reader. John Bunyan's *Pilgrim's Progress* was one such book, uniting story, philosophy, faith, imagination, theology and fun, with a certain amount of political insight thrown in. Gill Rowell's *CyberCindy* might not have quite the range of interests as Bunyan's *Pilgrim* but can certainly be placed in the same category. I first read the prototype of part of this book when it was submitted as a third year project at London Bible College. I was excited about it then and I am even more excited about the more developed work.

You could read it simply as a good story – with elements of history, adventure, science fiction, romance, fantasy and very perceptive analysis of character.

You could read it as an elucidation and critique of post-modern society providing perceptive insights into twenty-first century philosophical and sociological thinking.

You could read it as a creative commentary on two well-known Bible stories – concerning Ruth in the Old Testament and the Samaritan woman in the New Testament – illuminating and expounding the text.

You could read it as the description of a spiritual journey – challenging every reader to examine his or her own perceptions about faith and truth.

But let the reader beware. Almost as much as readers of *Pilgrim's Progress*, those who travel with *CyberCindy* are likely to find themselves rethinking their ideas; about themselves, about the world in which they live and about God and his place in their lives. You may never be the same again.

Mary Evans

Then Agrippa said to Paul, 'Do you think that in such a short time you can persuade me to be a Christian?'

Paul replied, 'Short time or long – I pray God that not only you but all who are listening to me today may become what I am, except for these chains' (Acts 26:28–29).

An old lady on a wet and windy track, the mud sticky and soft about her feet. Her frame is bent with age; the wind blows her from behind and pushes down against her back, billowing about her body, every step an achievement, a small victory. The woman's body is forced to kow-tow to the elements, her skirt, a deep, rusty red, swirls around her legs, revealing thick heavy boots. A black shawl flaps against the woman's shoulders, held there by the grip of her large, gnarled fingers, one hand firmly grasping the shawl, the other hand leaning dependently on a walking stick.

A single woman on a single track.

A great expanse of countryside sweeps around her on all sides, formidable in its misery. Just to the side of the road, ahead, is a large, dark tree, its branches, leafless and angular, brutally jutting into the skyline. Dark, tempestuous clouds gather high in the sky, an omen to the coming storm. Yet in the midst of the heavy black clouds is a tiny patch of light blue sky. CyberCindy stares at the patch of blue, mesmerised. She wonders why the artist put it there, so incongruous on an otherwise bleak scene.

Let's Communicate!

If you wish to communicate,
On this one thing please meditate:
Avoid pretence, be real, be true,
That I might know who's really you.
Show me yourself in honesty,
And not the you you'd have me see.
We will not progress very far,
Unless you show me who you are.
Yet all is lost if you don't see
The person who is really me![1]

The Engineer smiled to herself. As she smiled, she lurched forward and picked up a large book hidden under a pile of smaller books on her untidy desk. The book felt peculiar in her hands; she was not familiar with it and yet accepted that, for some people, the book was so vital they had been willing to die for the words that it contained. She flicked through the pages excitedly, until she found what she wanted to read, her tongue finding rest on her bottom lip as it always did when she was engrossed:

> In the days when the judges ruled, there was a famine in the land, and a man from Bethlehem in Judah, together with her wife and two sons, went to live for a while in the country of Moab ... (Ruth 1:1).

She paused momentarily.

Her eyes looked at the print before her, but they weren't engaging with it. The task she had just accepted from Lucy Watkins (Director of a newly formed company named Existentialist Virtual Worlds) was the most challenging one she had ever embraced. She appreciated that it would mean a lot of hard work; that the landscaping would need to be accurate, that the character formation was going to be something of a headache. But it was difficult to conceive of any other project with which she had been involved which was potentially as significant as this could turn out to be. There would be technical difficulties of course, but that was not where the real challenge was. The key issue would be in understanding how the historical, theological and cultural aspects of both worlds could interact. If she hashed this up her reputation would plummet; she would become a laughing stock. If she succeeded, well ...

There would be four phases to The Project. The first would be to know the story inside out. The second phase would be to get as much information as possible on

1

background – history, geography, cultural norms and so on, to give the setting integrity and ensure it was educationally sound. The third would be to recreate the characters as true to the original as possible. She would need a lot of help from psychologists and behavioural experts, as well as theologians, Jews and Christians. And the fourth stage – the most difficult from a technical perspective – would be to enable the world she was creating to relate to the world which would be investigating it.

A good team was essential: experts from every field would be paramount if The Project was going to have any credibility at all. She thought of Bill Williams, Cliff Coley, Sinead Smith. She wanted any aspect a cybernaut may wish to investigate to be available, just for the asking.

So nothing must be left unnoticed, no aspect ungrasped or untouched. Indeed, if she was to be faithful to The Project, attention to every detail was vital to success. And the Engineer wanted success because it was this project, above all others to date, which would secure her reputation and eminence in the field in which she worked. This was going to be the most viable and authentic virtual world available in Net history.

Initially, she had resisted the invitation because Lucy had been resolute on the world she was asking the Engineer to create: it was the world of the biblical character, Ruth. The Engineer had seen no merit or attraction, no good reason to recreate such a Bible world. In her opinion, the Bible was boring. She would much rather have been involved with fantasy and entertainment – innovative world creation – seascapes, monster worlds, out-of-this-world experiences, that sort of thing. But Lucy (who the Engineer suspected of being a Christian, although she had never come out and confessed it) had argued her case powerfully. No other book had sold as many copies in the world as the Bible; once hooked the potential for hours of online engagement and interaction was enormous (for spiritual adventure was always ongoing), and once a cybernaut's appetite for things spiritual had been whetted she was sure that they would have travellers dipping in and out of these virtual worlds for life.

The key element would be interaction, relationship.

Lucy wanted the Bible characters to argue their point of view with today's surfers. She wanted interaction that embraced the emotions, the senses, as well as the intellect – a holistic experience for the whole person.

Lucy felt that to create a Bible character, to create a persona that would accurately reflect the one found in the pages of the Bible was an immense challenge. And she wanted that Bible character to speak into today's world. It would, she had asserted, be almost as good as time travel. Lucy had been so positive that The Project could work, but had also emphasised how crucial it was to offer excellence. It was far more demanding than creating an illusory imaginary world, she argued, for the prospect of simulating a world which had once been real was far greater than making something fictitious out of current knowledge and technology. This project would present real challenges, real hurdles to overcome. So it needed someone good. And the Engineer, Lucy had said, smiling at her, was good.

The Engineer knew nothing of Ruth's story to begin with. She wasn't religious. Belief in God didn't much bother her either way. But she was ambitious, and she found the challenge of the task irresistible. There was no doubt that the future lay in space creation – cyberspace offered freedom and eternity; it offered communication and interconnectedness; it offered community and relationship. And here she was ... right at the heart of it.

Could anything else be more satisfying?

PART
ONE

blue

CyberCindy opens her eyes, having realised that for the past ten minutes or so she has been concentrating on trying to keep them shut. The morning light is dusky and not dark; she listens to the cars passing by outside, the hum of a lorry waiting at traffic lights, and reluctantly turns to her bedside table, reaching out for the clock. It's 09:45 hrs. She leans back on her pillow and shuts her eyes. What will today bring? It's just another day. She turns over and snuggles up in her duvet.

CyberCindy is bored.

(The narrative is related in the present tense, because the present is all that concerns the truly postmodern individual.)

She stays in bed until midday, getting up only because she needs to pee, and then makes herself a cup of coffee.

> It is impossible to discern, in that fragrant cup of coffee, the misery of the underpaid Brazilian bean-picker's family.[2]

She strolls over to her computer and switches it on.

> Electronic media is the supreme postmodernist art form. Entertainment without energy. It is vast in its potential, immediate and visual – effortless fun. By contrast, reading requires the engagement of the imagination, abstract thought, the connection of sequential

ideas and an inner life. Once reading disappears then anti-intellectualism, relativism and shallowness accelerate.[3] That is why CyberCindy is bored; she is a product of her age. She lives for today, and today nothing is happening in her life.

Her computer boots up and as it does so it says, 'Good morning, CyberCindy. How lovely you're looking today.'

'You don't really mean that,' CyberCindy says, nonchalantly, crossing her legs and supping at her coffee, turning towards the screen, which gives no reply until it offers her various program options in its dull monotonous voice. The Internet, usually a source of inspiration and delight, gives CyberCindy lots of choices, but today she is unimpressed. She gazes dispassionately at the screen as the machine, which she has affectionately named Toby, awaits her command. Her eyes scan the menus; her fingers tap impatiently on the desk.

'Paranormal' catches her eye. Interesting.

'I wonder ...,' she muses.

'Paranormal, Toby,' she says to the screen. The computer remains dormant for a few seconds, and then announces, 'Command unclear. Please repeat.'

CyberCindy swears under her breath, and says very loudly and clearly, 'Pa-ra-normal, Toby dear.' She sits and watches the word on the screen slowly fragment into pieces and then into grey dots. The screen goes blank and then reforms, offering more choice. *Aromatherapy ... Astrology ... Buddhism ... Bahaism ... Christianity ... Dreamwork ... Feng Shui ... Herbalism ... Hinduism ... Human Potential ... Ching ... Islam ... Meditation ...*

Mysticism ... Psychosynthesis ... Spiritualism ...
Transcendental Meditation ... Sufism ... Zen ...

CyberCindy's spiritual adventure has begun.

She shuts her eyes and, annoyed with Toby's response to
her this morning, opts for touch control rather than voice
activation. She touches the screen. It's cool and hard; her
finger is smooth and warm. Technology and flesh fuse,
and in that simple movement CyberCindy makes herself
vulnerable to an unknown future-fate may do with her
what it will.

She is presented with another menu – Anglo-catholic,
Baptist, Conservative, Charismatic, Evangelical, Feminist,
Gay, House Church, Greek Orthodox, Liberal,
Reformed, Roman Catholic – and realises to her dismay
that she must have hit on Christianity. Her impression of
Christians is that they are moralistic and lacking in fun.
To find Christianity under Paranormal is not her idea of
accurate indexing. However, she can't be bothered to
exit, and doesn't feel inclined to make more decisions, so
perseveres. She touches 'Bible' and is given further
choice: Genesis, Exodus, Leviticus, Numbers,
Deuteronomy, Joshua, Judges, Ruth, 1 Samuel, 2 Samuel
... her eyes dart back to Ruth. Ruth? What is a woman's
name doing on the index? Who is Ruth? CyberCindy is
momentarily intrigued. She has understood Christianity
to be a male dominated religion, with a male god.

So God created man in his own image, in the image of God he
created him; male and female he created them (Genesis 1:27).

> The woman herself alone is not the image of God: whereas the man alone is the image of God as fully and completely as when the woman is joined with him.[4]

> It is idolatrous to make males more 'like God' than females ... All categories of classical theology have been distorted by androcentrism, which makes the male normative in a way that reduces women to invisibility.[5]

The Roman Catholic and the Greek Orthodox Church are firm in their resolve to keep women out of leadership in the church on the grounds that Father God is male, Jesus Christ the Saviour is male, the twelve chosen apostles were male, and therefore only a male can truly represent God. It is only relatively recently (11 November 1992) that the Church of England recognised the ordination of women, and non-conformist churches have opposing views on the subject. Male leadership, which almost invariably interprets the Scriptures in a way that may exacerbate or in any case continue the division and polarisation of gender roles, dominates the worldwide church.[6]

Feminism has often been rejected because it is seen to devalue the family, but this could also be said of all believers, male or female (see Matthew 10:34–39). For the believer, God takes precedence over all. The issue for today's church is what it means to submit? For centuries pulpit preachers have emphasised the need for wives to submit to their husbands, with scant attention paid to the corresponding need for husbands to submit to Christ. In a postmodern world, where male/female roles are no longer clearly defined, submission needs clear interpretation, for it has little to do with gender roles. The Christian ideal is for all to live in submission to Christ, and we are told to submit to one another (Ephesians 5:21). Traditionally women are the homemakers, and men are the breadwinners – but there is no biblical precedence for this. Submission is to do with attitude, not function, or roles. Jesus challenges cultural conventions, restoring dignity and worth to both male and female, whatever their social status.

The church, of all institutions in the world, should have been the first to dispense with roles in terms of gender, and emphasised them in terms of gifting. Male and female are equal in status from God's perspective: they complement one another because they are different.

> Post-evangelicals, for the most part, are heirs to a...post-feminist culture. They assume sexual equality and take for granted the right of a woman to follow a career. They have no reservations about house-husbands, if that is what both partners agree, and they see no reason why men should be in charge; roles are a matter of arrangement.[7]

CyberCindy presses her finger hard on the short feminine name – Ruth – and waits. Her browser takes its time. CyberCindy is frustrated. She adds more sugar to her coffee while she waits.

'Toby, you're taking too long this morning,' she tells the machine.

'Please wait,' it replies.

CyberCindy determines that her next major task will be to upgrade her hardware. Whilst she is absent-mindedly thinking about this, the screen on her desk goes through a series of colourful displays which advocate daily reading of the Scriptures, talking with God, praising the Lord and such like, accompanied by loud rhythmic music. Then suddenly the screen goes black, the music stops, and for a moment CyberCindy thinks her equipment has gone down, until she notices, in the bottom left-hand corner, a tiny spot of light begin to glow. She watches it gradually evolve into a brightly coloured rainbow stretching across the screen. The rainbow then curls in upon itself, and shapes itself into an arrow, which shoots quickly towards the word RUTH, which has appeared in bold red in the top left-hand corner, and grows until it fills the screen. CyberCindy waits for the download to complete. Something in her unconscious can't quite believe she is doing this. Next follows a subtitle, simultaneously accompanied with a soft feminine voice, mellow and warm: 'A story about providence'.

'Providence? What the hell's that?', she thinks to herself, but remains silent, her curiosity still engaged.

? *Western ideas formerly embraced the notion of providence, that all things in heaven and earth were known by, and controlled by, God. During the Age of Reason this developed into a philosophy that society was getting better; that the human race was progressing to a brighter future. But the late twentieth century became disenchanted with rational knowledge, for in this century alone more people have been killed than in all previous periods.*

12

There has been a definite shift towards nihilism – the rejection of all religious and moral principles.

CyberCindy opts to skip all the factual stuff concerning dating and author and purpose by pressing a fast-forward symbol in the right-hand corner of the screen, and goes straight to Chapter 1, which she assumes is where the story begins.

'Go ahead,' she says, and the story begins …

Accompanied by words with gorgeous artwork in the background, a new picture evolving by degrees and replacing the previous one every so often, the mellow voice starts in confident tones, 'In the days when the judges ruled …'

Reader, choose to:

F1 fast-forward to page 29[8]
F2 read the Old Testament book of Ruth in your own Bible;[9]
F3 read the story below.[10]

Ruth's Story: Chapter 1

Long, long ago (over 3,000 years), in the days before there was any king ruling over Israel, during the time when the people were led by judges, there was a famine.[11] So great was the famine, and so desperate were the people for food, that a man who lived in Bethlehem, Judah (the same town in which King David was born, and later, Jesus Christ, the Messiah) decided to go in search of food in the country of Moab.

This particular family were Ephrathites, and Ephrathites in Bethlehem at that time were people of standing (so far as we can tell). They were wealthy folk, who could wield power and authority in the community. But famine is no respecter of status, and the family, wealthy or not, had empty bellies and hungry hearts. The father, whose name was 'My God is King' (or Elimelech, in ancient Hebrew – a strange name for a man, it is true), forsook the protection of his clan and tribe in favour of feeding his wife and their two sons. His sons were frail and sickly. They needed feeding up. In them lay hope for the future. They would continue My God is King's family line; they would care for My God is King's wife; they were rather like insurance policies for they secured a stable future. So wealthy or not, in search of bread, My God is King set out for Moab, a land of plenty, together with his wife 'Delightful' (Naomi) and his two frail sons, 'To-Be-Sick' (Mahlon) and 'Annihilation' (Kilion). My God is King didn't plan to stay in Moab forever, but he did plan to stay for a while, until the famine was over. And so it was that the family left Bethlehem in Judah over 1000 years before Jesus was born there. The sun was shining; the air was hot; and though the lips of everyone were dry, their eyes were wet with tears of hunger.

Strictly speaking, Moab was enemy country. During the exodus the Moabites had refused to give the Israelites food as they had travelled through on their way to the Promised Land. As a result, they were a cursed people.[12] Not only that, the Moabites worshipped many gods, (unlike the monotheistic Israelites), although they did have a favourite god, called Chemosh. Sometimes Moabites were called

14

'The People of Chemosh'. Not only that. Moabites were descended from Lot's incest with his daughters. His daughters, fearful that their family line would die out (and because there were no other men around at the time), made Lot drunk and then made babies with him.[13] Not only that, Moabite women had a reputation for leading the Israelites astray and tempting them away from the one true God to worship the things of this world – sex and wealth and other gods.[14]

So, it is rather strange that My God is King left Bethlehem in Judah and went to live in Moab amongst the heathens.[15] But when you are starving, and when your lovely, charming wife is starving and when your sickly boys are starving, it may be that it is food and not favour that one seeks.

So My God is King went to Moab with his family and found food there. But before very long (we do not know how long) My God is King died, leaving Delightful and To-Be-Sick and Annihilation to fend for themselves, which they did.

When the boys were old enough, To-Be-Sick married a Moabite woman named 'Friend' (Ruth) and Annihilation married a Moabite woman named 'Stiff Necked' (Orpah). We cannot be sure, but rumour has it that in marrying these women, the Israelite men were paid land as a dowry, land which they could farm for food. And so it was that Delightful was provided for after My God is King died. For ten years her sons and her daughters-in-law cared for her. Then tragedy fell. To-Be-Sick and Annihilation (true to their names and true to their destiny) died, leaving Delightful devastated, destitute and diminished.[16]

15

One day, Delightful heard that Yahweh had come to the aid of his people (the Israelites) by providing food for them. So she prepared to return to Bethlehem, together with her daughters-in-law. Accompanied by them, Delightful left the place where she had been living, which some folk might have called home, but which, for Delightful was not home because it was not Bethlehem, and took the road that would eventually lead them back to the land of Judah, the land of her roots, the land of protection, the land of clan and tribe, and most important of all, the land of food.

(Yahweh: a form of the Hebrew name of God. The name came to be regarded by Jews [c. 300 BC] as too sacred to be spoken.)

As the journey began, Delightful's awful predicament lay heavily on her weary and fearful heart. One vulnerable woman is better than three, she thought. The famine was over, and that was good. But Delightful knew that she would need what My God is King thought he could do without: protection. She decided that her daughters-in-law would be better provided for in Moab than in Judah. What Israelite man would care for them? They are Moabites; they are barren, proving themselves to be a useless commodity; their men-folk die on them. This is hardly a good advertisement for marriage. There will be no man to barter for them, no man to argue their case, no man to give them worth. At least, if they return to their mother's home they will come under the protection of their father. Skivvying for their brothers' wives would surely be better than having no brothers' wives to skivvy for.

16

So Delightful turned to her daughters-in-law and said to them, 'You girls go home to your mother's home, now, and may Yahweh be as kind and generous to you as you have been to my sons and me. Perhaps, if Yahweh is kind to you, you will each find another husband.'

At this the women wept and kissed one another, for they were full of pity at their dire circumstance – pity for themselves, pity for one another. But Friend and Stiff Necked refused to abandon Delightful, and insisted that they would return with her to her people. For they knew that Delightful, who was so much older than they, was also so much more vulnerable.

But Delightful was stubborn. She implored them to return home. She could not give them any security; and their arrival with her in Bethlehem would be sheer madness. They would be used and abused; whatever status they had as My God is King's daughters-in-law or his sons wives is dubious now that their men-folk are dead. There was no man to defend them; and Delightful was unable to guarantee marriages for them. Even if she were to find a husband for herself (unlikely), and even if she could still bear babies and provide husbands for Friend and Stiff-Necked from her own old body (unlikely), who would care for the women in the meantime? In any case, were she able to give birth to two baby boys, by the time they grew up, Friend and Stiff-Necked would be too old to bear babies by them. So Elimelech's line would still be no more.

'My lot is much worse than yours,' Delightful told her daughters-in-law, 'for Yahweh has turned against me. I won't find another husband, but you still have a chance, so return home and find husbands for yourselves, with God's help.'

The women wept again, and Stiff-Necked, who realised the awful truth of her mother-in-law's argument, returned home, after kissing Delightful goodbye. But Friend would not abandon Delightful to a solitary future. She clung to Delightful, refusing to leave her.

'Look,' Delightful said, 'Your sister-in-law is going back to her people and her gods. You go back with her.'

But Friend replied, 'Don't you dare implore me to leave you or to turn away from you. Wherever you go, I will go with you. Wherever you stay, I will stay with you. Your people will be my people. Your God will be my God. Where you die, I will die, and I will be buried beside you. May Yahweh deal with me very severely if anything but death separates me from you.'

Friend had decided she would be Delightful's protector and provider, with the help of Delightful's God, and nothing but death would get in her way.

Friend's outburst silenced Delightful and the women travelled on through dusty, parched terrain, on and on, until they came to the town of their destination, Bethlehem.[17] On their arrival, the whole town was hot with gossip. Delightful's sad and tragic story is the focus of conversation at the town gate, the well, the market, everywhere. The women muttered to one another in disbelief, 'Can this really be the same Delightful who left all those years ago with My God is King?'

And Delightful, who saw their eyes resting on her in awe, said to the women, 'Don't call me Delightful, call me "Bitter" (Mara), because God the Almighty has made my life bitter. Yahweh has judged against me, he has finished off my family and with it my future.' And Delightful, whose life was once full of hope in hungry times is now full of despair in times of plenty, and in her anguish she fails to see the friend that Yahweh has given her in Friend. For whilst neither woman had any choice concerning their menfolk's demise, Friend voluntarily chose to abandon her own family, her own country and her own friends to enter Delightful's world. Friend, a young Moabite woman, with no status, a foreigner and a widow, was by her side but got no mention, even though she had chosen to stick by her mother-in-law until one of them died.[18]

And so it was that Delightful-who-was-now-Bitter returned from Moab, accompanied by Friend, the Moabitess, her daughter-in-law, and arrived in Bethlehem just as the barley harvest was beginning.

The telephone rings. CyberCindy is immediately distracted from the story, pleased that someone has rung her. 'Wait', she shouts loudly. The voice stops and the screen is still. She presses a button on the mobile, a small colourful tube wrapped around her wrist. 'Yeah?', she answers, almost flippantly, 'What is it?'

'You're out of bed, then.' It's Carl, her brother.

'What's it to you?'

'Shall we meet up tonight?'

'I've got nothing better to do.'

'Great. I'll come round then. See ya, gorgeous.'

A bleep, a flash of red, and the conversation is finished. She returns to the screen.

'Go', she commands, almost dramatically.

Ruth's Story: Chapter 2

Now it just so happened that Delightful-who-was-now-Bitter had a relative on her husband's side, from the clan of My God is King, a man of good reputation and standing, whose name was Strong Warrior. He was a landowner and farmer.

Soon after Delightful-who-was-now-Bitter and Friend, the Moabitess, arrived in Bethlehem, Friend said to Delightful-who-was-now-Bitter, 'Shall I go to the fields and join the harvesters, picking up the leftover grain behind anyone who lets me?'[19] And Delightful-who-was-now-Bitter, said, 'Yes, my daughter! Do it! Do it now!' for both the women were very hungry. Delightful-who-was-now-Bitter didn't accompany her daughter-in-law to the field. Though she walked the journey from Moab to Judah, she felt old and weary now. She had already suffered one humiliation in returning to Bethlehem destitute, having left it with a certain status. She could not bear the thought of publicly subjecting herself to the taunts, in look or words, of harvesters as she strives to glean food from a field that in the past decade had not yielded a crop sufficient enough for her needs, and which she and her husband had rejected.

So, with Delightful-who-was-now-Bitter's approval, Friend went out and began to glean in the fields behind the harvesters. As it so happened, she worked in a field belonging to Strong Warrior, that same Strong Warrior who was from Elimelech's clan.

Presently, Strong Warrior arrived from Bethlehem (for the fields were on the outskirts of the town), and greeted his workers.

'Yahweh be with you!', he called

'Yahweh bless you!', returned the workers.

Then Strong Warrior, curious to see someone he didn't know working on his patch, asked his foreman 'Whose young woman is that?' (Strong Warrior had a right to know what cause his diminishing profits were aiding and wanted to know what man, if any, was responsible for Friend, and what man she was answerable to. He wanted to be sure she was genuinely needy.)

The foreman answered, 'She is the Moabitess who came back from Moab with Delightful. She asked me if she could glean behind the harvesters, and I gave her permission. She went into the field early this morning and hasn't stopped, except for a short rest in the shelter.'

Strong Warrior went over to Friend and said to her, 'Listen to me, my dear. Don't glean anywhere else, but stay here with my servant girls. Watch where the men harvest, and follow along after the girls. I have told the men not harm you, or shout abuse at you. Whenever you are thirsty, you just go and help yourself from the water jars the men have filled.'

At this unexpected generosity, Friend fell down on the ground before Strong Warrior. She asked, 'How come you are so kind to me, a stranger and a foreigner?'

Strong Warrior replied, 'I have heard all about what you have done for your mother-in-law since your husband died – how you left your parents and your homeland and came to live with a people you didn't know. I know that you left everything to look after Delightful. So may Yahweh shower blessings upon you for what you have done. May you be richly rewarded by him, the God of Israel, under whose wings you have come to take refuge.'

Friend, who has sought to protect Delightful, thinks Strong Warrior rather poetic, and is flattered to see that for some reason her protection is his concern.

(NB: Strong Warrior doesn't mention that he is a kinsman redeemer.)

'May you always think so highly of me, sir,' says Friend, 'You have been so generous and so kind – even though I am the least of the least and don't even have the standing of one of your servant girls.'[20]

At lunchtime, Strong Warrior calls Friend over to join him and offers her bread and wine vinegar. When she sits down with the workers, Strong Warrior gives her some roasted grain and after she has eaten all that she can, there is still lots left over. As she gets up to continue gleaning, Strong Warrior orders his men 'Even if she oversteps the mark and gathers among the sheaves, don't embarrass her. Leave her plenty to gather from the bundles. Make it easy for her, and be generous with her. And no hanky-panky – you'll have me to answer to if you show her any disrespect!'

So Friend gleaned in the field until evening. Then she threshed the barley she had gathered, and it amounted to about four gallons. Tired, but satisfied at such a good days work, Friend carried her harvest back to Bethlehem, and her mother-in-law was amazed. Not only had Friend gathered so much barley, she also brought out her leftovers from lunchtime for Delightful-who-is-now-Bitter to eat.

Delightful-who-is-now-Bitter asked her, 'Where on earth did you glean today? May God bless the man who looked after you!', for she knows that the only way Friend could have gleaned so much barley would be through the favour of the land owner in whose field she had worked. She had not expected Friend to come back with more than a handful of grain (and possibly a soiled reputation) if she had been lucky, and an empty stomach and bruised feelings if she had not.

Then Friend told her mother-in-law, 'I worked in Strong Warrior's field today.'

'May Yahweh bless him,' Delightful-who-is-now-Bitter responded, 'for he has not stopped doing good to the living and the dead!'[21] She added, 'Strong Warrior is a close relative of ours, on My God is King's side of the family; he is one of our family redeemers.'[22]

Friend the Moabitess continued, 'He even told me to stay with his workers until the harvest is finished.'

Delightful-who-is-now-Bitter said to Friend her daughter-in-law, 'That's a good idea, stay with his girls, because in someone else's field you might get hurt. Not everyone is as benevolent as Strong Warrior.' Delightful-who-is-now-Bitter perceives that Friend has won the protection of a male within her husband's clan; it is only prudent to take advantage of this protection. The news of Strong Warrior's generosity is sweet music to her ears; even now an idea is taking root in her restless mind, an idea which could, if all goes well, prove beneficial to everyone.

Friend, true to her word, stayed close to the servant girls of Strong Warrior and gleaned the fields until both the barley and the wheat harvests were finished, continuing to live with her mother-in-law.

Ruth's Story: Chapter 3

One day, as the harvesting was coming to an end, Delightful-who-is-now-Bitter, Friend's mother-in-law, said to Friend, 'My dear, I think I should try to find a home for you, where you will be well provided for. Strong Warrior, with whose servant girls you have been, is a member of our clan. I think we should be able to call on him to help us. Tonight he will be winnowing barley on the threshing-floor. Get dressed up and make yourself beautiful. Then go down to the threshing-floor, but don't let him see you. After he has finished eating and drinking watch where he lies down. Then go quietly over and uncover his feet and lie down. He will tell you what to do.'[23]

'I will do what you say,' Friend responds. So Friend went down to the threshing floor and did everything her mother-in-law told her to do.

When Strong Warrior had finished eating and drinking, and was in a good mood, he went to lie down at the far end of the grain pile.

Ping! A symbol bursts into the corner of the screen. Someone has just sent her an e-mail. It is tempting to go and look at it, but CyberCindy wants to know what will happen next. The e-mail can wait.

Friend approached quietly, uncovered his feet and lay down.[24] Then she waited. And waited. In the middle of the night something startled Strong Warrior, and he turned round violently, only to discover a woman lying at his feet.

'Who are you?', he asked.

'I am your servant, Friend,' Friend said 'I have come to you seeking help. Would you spread the corner of your garment over me, since you are our family redeemer?'[25]

'May Yahweh bless you, my daughter!', says Strong Warrior, 'For by coming to me now you are even more generous in your actions than you were before, when you left everything behind in Moab to look after Delightful. You haven't chased after younger men, rich or poor. You have come to me, a member of your husband's family, for you wish to honour him and his clan. And I am grateful for that, because his clan is my clan. So don't be afraid. I will do everything you want me to. Everyone in the town respects you. But although it is true that I am near of kin, there is another man who is nearer in line to To-Be-Sick than I am. Stay here now and in the morning I will find out what he wants to do. If he wants to redeem, good; let him redeem. But if he is not willing, as surely as the Lord lives, then I will. Lie here until the morning.'

So Friend lay there until early morning, and in the grey light of dawn arose before anyone could be recognised. Strong Warrior was keen that no-one should know of Friend's visit. He wanted it kept a secret. He said to her, 'Don't let anyone know that a woman came to the threshing floor.' Then he said to Friend, 'Hold out the shawl you are wearing'. Friend did so, and Strong Warrior poured six measures of barley into it and then tied it to her back before going back to town.

On seeing Friend, Delightful-who-is-now-Bitter could hardly contain herself, and greeted her daughter-in-law asking, 'What happened, my daughter? Tell me all about it!'

Then Friend told her everything that Strong Warrior had said, adding, 'He gave me these six measures of barley, so that I wouldn't come back to you empty handed.' On seeing the barley, Delightful-who-is-now-Bitter said, 'Now we must wait, my daughter, and see what happens. For Strong Warrior will not rest until the matter is settled today.'

Ruth's Story: Chapter 4

Meanwhile, Boaz went to the town gate where legal transactions and business was carried out, and sat there, waiting to call a meeting. When the nearest next of kin, the family-redeemer – a man with no name – came along, Strong Warrior said, 'Come over here, my friend, and sit down.' So the man went over there and sat down.

Then Strong Warrior took ten of the elders of the town (similar to members of a town council) and said 'Sit here', and they sat there. Then Strong Warrior got on with the business. He said to the Man with No Name, 'Delightful-who-is-now-Bitter, who has come back from Moab, is selling the piece of land that belonged to our brother, My God is King. I thought I should let you know so that you can buy it in the presence of the elders. If you will redeem it, then do so. But if you won't, tell me, so that I can redeem it. For no-one has the right to redeem except you, and after you, I am next in line.'

'I will redeem it,' said the Man With No Name.

Then Strong Warrior said, 'On the day you buy the land from Delightful-who-is-now-Bitter and from Friend the Moabitess, you will also acquire the dead man's widow so that his name is kept with his property.'

At this, the Man with No Name, said 'If I acquire Delightful and Friend when I redeem the land, then I don't want it because I might loose my own estate. I can't do it. You redeem it yourself if you want to. I cannot do it.'[26]

So the Man with No Name said to Strong Warrior, 'You buy it,' and he removed his sandal, thus giving up his right to redeem the land and passing it to Strong Warrior.

(Now in those long ago days in Israel, the way legal transactions were made final for the redemption and transfer of property was that one party took off his sandal and gave it to the other.)

Then Strong Warrior announced to the elders and all the people, 'Today you are witnesses that I have bought from Delightful all the property of My God is King, Annihilation and To-Be-Sick, and have acquired Friend the Moabitess, To-Be-Sick's widow, as my wife. This will keep his name with the property, so that it will not disappear from among his family or from the town records. Today you are witnesses!'[27]

Then the elders and everyone gathered at the gate conferred blessing on the arrangement and said, 'Yes, we are witnesses. May Yahweh make your new wife like Rachel and Leah, who between them built up the house of Israel.[28] May you be honoured and respected in Ephrathah and be famous in Bethlehem for what you have done, a good example for everyone. And through the offspring that Yahweh gives you by this young woman, may your family be like that of Perez, whom Tamar bore to Judah.'[29]

So Strong Warrior took Friend and she became his wife. Then they slept together, and Yahweh enabled her to conceive, and she gave birth to a boy. The women said to Delightful, who was no longer Bitter, 'Praise be to Yahweh, who didn't leave you without a family redeemer, a boy to keep the family name going. May he become famous throughout Israel! He will give you new energy and keep you going in your old age. For your daughter-in-law, who loves you and who is better to you than seven sons, has given him birth.'

Then Delightful who is truly delighted took the child, and nursed him. The women said in praise and pleasure, 'Delightful has a son!' Whoever would have thought that Delightful's fortunes would have been restored? And they named the baby boy 'Servant' (Obed). He became the father of Jesse, the father of David.

This then is the family line of Perez:

Perez was the father of Hezron, Hezron the father of Ram, Ram the father of Amminadab, Amminadab the father of Nahshon, Nahshon the father of Salmon, Salmon the father of Boaz, Boaz the father of Obed, Obed the father of Jesse and Jesse the father of David.

THE END

CyberCindy sups her coffee. She had not expected to find a story, and a love story at that, in the Bible. Her machine makes an unexpected announcement, 'Ruth is available in virtual reality. Consult your nearest transfer station for further details.'

'Mmm,' she says to herself, glancing at her watch, 'I wonder ...'.

She goes to her wardrobe and pulls out her SceneSensa, her Grips and her Rompacomp, which has been hanging dormant like an empty snakeskin, waiting occupancy to bring it to life.

(Rompacomp: customised computer clothing.)

She pulls off her clothes, and her bare legs carefully step into the futuristic clothing, a heavy garment not unlike a boiler suit. She pulls it up around her waist and then over her shoulders, making sure she doesn't damage any of the fibre-optic cells, as her arms slide into the sleeves. She seals the outfit and strokes her body to make sure that all the sensors will connect with her skin.

(Grips: sensory gloves that enable CyberCindy to send commands and receive signals at the flick of a finger or a wave of the hand. The SceneSensa enables CyberCindy to experience visually the virtual world she has entered; it engulfs the top part of her head completely, so that she sees and hears only what her virtual world offers, whilst breathing the surrounding air in her flat. It is like living in a three dimensional movie. At any time CyberCindy can revert to the real world.)

? *CyberCindy normally wears her Rompacomp to log into the fibre-optic network she uses for work. This enables her to engage with her colleagues throughout the world whilst never leaving her flat. CyberCindy is one of many* *consultants employed to determine the feasibility of corporate virtual business. She has no set pattern for work, but organises her own work schedule and so long as her tasks are completed according to budget, no one checks up on her hours.*

When wearing her Rompacomp, she can talk, hear and see her colleagues; she can shake hands with them, laugh with them and generally manoeuvre nearly as naturally as in real life. She can share her creative ideas with them immediately, conversing freely. She frequently has brainstorming and planning sessions with other folk in her line of business. (If CyberCindy wanted to, she could hug her colleagues too, but she is not given to displaying her emotions.) She can travel to any work zone for which she is legally registered. She has a personal identification number (PIN), which allows immediate access to those professional contacts approved of by her company.

The World Wide Web was the tip of the iceberg; the Internet the start of a whole new playground, a new world, and with the advances in technology which have made virtual reality a real aspect of early twenty-first-century life, CyberCindy is ambitious to be at the forefront of this technological revolution. She has perceived that with the coming of virtual reality the world can become a bigger place; there will be no limit to the space which can be created. Technology is moving so fast that physical production cannot keep a pace; but CyberCindy has no doubt that the future for commerce and entertainment can be found via the virtual worlds created through computer networking. She has unlimited access to limitless worlds, an interconnectedness with others which both fascinates and stimulates her desire for excitement.

CyberCindy doesn't speak to her neighbours in the flat next door or below her, and she doesn't expect them to speak to her. She watches television when she isn't surfing, or goes to her local gym, because she wants her body to be beautiful and strong. But it is the world of virtual reality that stimulates her the most. She feels as if she is living in a movie when she is travelling in cyberspace – adventures begin and unfold unceremoniously and she encounters people she would otherwise never meet, people who are unthreatening because she can terminate her relationship with them at any time she pleases.

So far CyberCindy has never used her Rompacomp for anything other than work, but today she wonders if her access number will allow her to navigate through Cyberspace for recreational purposes.

She likes her Rompacomp. It is in shades of purple and is customised to her body. It fits her perfectly. She makes sure that she has put it on properly by plugging in to the Safety-net Valve on her hardware box. She gets the green light and the happy musical tone, and so turns to what she affectionately calls her Heartthrob, a pale neat box attached to the wall. She plugs her Rompacomp into it and turns a knob. As the system boots up she glances towards the clock by the sink. CyberCindy has a booking at the gym today for 15:30 hrs. She has two hours to get through before then. Her planned trip into another world is just the thing to while away the time.

red

CyberCindy puts the SceneSensa over her eyes and ears and gently presses the 'Go' button. When using the Internet, she still has to make certain decisions by way of menu charts, although in virtual reality these are presented more like London Underground maps than lists giving options. She chooses her first port of call, a local transfer station known as Gibson; it lights up to show that it has recognised her command. She settles down in her seat in front of her desk, which is situated in the corner of her flat, the fibre-optic nerves in her Rompacomp alive to the living nerves in her body. She touches a button; her journey begins.

I rise above and catch a timeline
Jet stream
north – south
west – east
I cannot see it
yet it sustains
and lifts
and thrusts me forward into space

So life ...
jet streaming
between
birth
and
death.
God holding both ends.[30]

> The illusion of travel serves to build a sense of continuous spatiality and transmits a sense of adventure to the cybernaut. Access is never really instantaneous, even with state of the art technology, and selecting paths, accessing different and distant computer networks constitutes a good deal of pleasure for the cyber traveller.[31]

The array of fast moving colours and lights reminds CyberCindy of the view of the lights of Piccadilly Circus she had as a little girl, sitting in the back of her mother's car, late at night. The merging sea of blurred ribbons and bright fluttering lights creates a tunnel that focuses her attention on the fast approaching transfer station. Her journey takes about half a minute and she finds herself entering a familiar large and busy place, not unlike an aeroplane hangar, littered with blue balls, which indicate the presence of other cyber travellers. A soft voice tells CyberCindy that she has reached her destination, and as the scene in front of her slows down and she comes to a halt, she looks around for a Bulletin Board.

(BBS: Bulletin Board System. A computer system accessible by modem where members can leave messages, send email, play games and trade files with other users.)

She locates one primarily by the cluster of balls surrounding it, and joins the throng, ready to see if she can access Ruth in a virtual world. She finds an empty space in front of a large white frame and taps into it, using the keyboard on her desk, her head witnessing a different world from her body. She types 'Any Bible freaks out there?' and waits for a response. It is not long before a smiling caricature of a face displays itself before her, boxed into the white frame.

'Hi there!', says the face, 'What d'you wanna know?'

CyberCindy says clearly, 'Address for Ruth.'

The smiley face blinks unemotionally, and after only a slight pause, answers, 'alt.bible.ot.Ruth@VR. Have a great time and thank the Lord for a lovely day!'

The caricature dissolves into a swirling marble on the screen. CyberCindy is just about to log the address into her routemaster when she feels someone tap her on the shoulder. However, she does not want to have an ad hoc conversation with anyone, so before she goes any further, she presses a small yellow square on her belt which communicates to other cyber travellers that she is present but not accessible (except in the case of an emergency, when her instruction would be overruled). The interceptor goes away, and CyberCindy logs the address into her computer and calls up a routemaster gopher. It tells her to access Ruth via Southbound Port. She looks at the map and sees that the most direct route will take ninety-four seconds, at high speed. Ages.

> On outward journeys, travel in cyberspace incurs cost to the traveller in proportion to the distance travelled. Homeward journeys are more direct; one can exit virtual reality almost immediately at any time.[32]

CyberCindy scans the station for signs and locates Southbound Port, whereupon she skids immediately up to it and, adjusting the light scanner on her SceneSensa to dim (for she is feeling strangely vulnerable and not inclined to experience brashness of hue or speed) she prepares for the next leg of her journey. She slides her international swipe card across the barrier post, which unlocks access to the Port. The barrier lights up so she dictates the address to a small microphone situated on her right.

A clear voice asks her by which mode she wishes to travel: air, earth, or water. She chooses air, and specifies self-flight, rather than jet aeroplane, helicopter, hovercraft, backpack, hot air balloon, the options are many. She likes the sensation of flying through cyberspace; it is her favourite form of transport. Having ascertained her medium of travel, the barrier swings wide, and CyberCindy begins her journey. She stands up, keeping her arms by her side, in Superman mode, and jets through the air at quite a pace, gently leaning to the left or right, occasionally pointing her head up to gain height, or down to survey the three-dimensional world unfolding beneath her, negotiating her way through new and unfamiliar territory.

When working, CyberCindy generally chooses to swim through the air, as this slows her speed a little and gives her more time to take in the scenery. But today she wants to arrive at her destination quickly; she is impatient and keen to see how the virtual world matches up with the one she has just experienced.

This leg of the journey has no view at the end of the tunnel, and no bright colours or lights. Rather, CyberCindy careers through a sea of swirling gentle greens and greys, occasional adverts for different software companies looming through the haze, and now and then she glimpses tall buildings and office blocks far away on the horizon, but as she gets closer they fade away, evolving into soft blue patches of colour, through which she continues to travel.

Gliding swiftly and determinedly through this abstract forest, CyberCindy wonders what she has let herself in for, and why the creator of this journey couldn't have been more imaginative. She is just thinking that the journey is overly long when, without warning, the imagery before her changes to a dull monochrome red, and immediately before her eyes she perceives a large, solid, wooden gate. She comes to a halt before it, and steadies her legs, gathering breath. Flying is great fun, but it can be quite exhausting too.

Written on the gate, in clear and brilliant yellow, and in a font which is unfamiliar to CyberCindy, is: RUTH.

Above the name are some hieroglyphics (which she later learns is Ruth written in Hebrew).

(Gate: This corresponds to the home page on a Web site; the welcome or index page.)

She scans the scene, but there is nothing else to see.

She tries to detect if other cybernauts are around, but her user-sensor only reports 'void'. She suddenly feels alone, a sensation that is alien and strange in cyberspace, although familiar in real life. Until now she has always viewed cyberspace as a busy metropolis of individuals, interacting and conversing with friends and strangers alike, everyone seeking their own satisfaction, following their own whim, but all somehow doing it together. The silence here causes her to panic, a long forgotten emotional phenomenon. CyberCindy presses 'Hold' to keep her presence at the threshold of Ruth and flips the control button on her visor: she sees her apartment. She sees her coffee cup on the desk, her unmade bed in the corner. She looks to the window and notices it is raining heavily. She relaxes and switches the control button once again, snaps her visor down over her head and focuses all her attention on the scene before her eyes.

The gate has a large iron handle.

CyberCindy steps forward and opens it. To her surprise, the gate creeks as her fingers firmly clasp and turn the handle.

indigo

As CyberCindy steps out into this new virtual world, she is met by a blast of warm air and hot blurred colours.

> *The Engineer has produced the virtual world of Ruth using a palette of around about sixteen million colours. Sophisticated pan and zoom features were used to customise the shape and size of the virtual world, and stereophonic sound outputs, using digital technology, create an illusion of intense, super-vivid hyper-reality.*

CyberCindy adjusts the focus knob on her visor.

She finds herself looking at a deep blue sky, the glare of the sun causing her to blink uncomfortably.

As she becomes accustomed to her surroundings, she realizes she is looking at a road, a hard dusty road, surrounded by barren land. Her overwhelming impression is of stark, dry earth and callous heat.

A little ahead of her are two women, dressed in black, walking slowly but deliberately, and beside each of them is a donkey, laden with bags.

She walks briskly to catch them up, and as she approaches them greets the women from behind with a loud and friendly, 'Hi!'

? *CyberCindy has already forgotten her unease of a few moments ago, and is now participating fully in the scene before her. She likes being in virtual reality, because she can manipulate her circumstances according to her own whims. She doesn't have to consider the likes or dislikes of anyone else; she is in command; she makes the choices; she is answerable to no one and yet the adventure is all prepared for her. She doesn't have to put any effort into it; she just receives what it gives. She can determine her destiny because she can choose to play or exit; to venture into a different world, and reject her current experience without any repercussions to do with broken relationships or agreements. She has perfect freedom.*

The younger of the two women turns to her and smiles gently. The older woman does not seem to notice CyberCindy at all.

Ruth does not look quite like CyberCindy expected her to look. She does not know what she expected; all she knows is that she is surprised by what she sees. The virtual reality Ruth does not match up to the Ruth in the story screen.

Ruth's eyes are very dark, and underneath them is a little sweep of skin which indicates lack of sleep, or worry. Her eyebrows are dark, and thick and heavy. Her skin, also dark, is already lined, even though she is only in her late twenties, and her nose is strong and well defined; it rather dominates her face, whilst Ruth's lips, which are small and thin, serve to punctuate it with precision and purpose. CyberCindy catches a glimpse of Ruth's hair (which is dark and which CyberCindy assumes is straight and long). It is covered with a black scarf, which drapes rather raggedly about her small shoulders. Ruth is smaller than CyberCindy anticipated, and she is certainly not what CyberCindy deems to be sexually attractive. Yet from those dark eyes there emanates a flicker of interest, of questioning, of something that CyberCindy can't quite fathom.

Ruth speaks, apparently unperturbed at CyberCindy's intrusion, 'I was hoping you might join me.' Her voice is warm and rich.

'Why is that?', CyberCindy asks, her interest aroused, surprised that Ruth is taking the initiative.

'Well,' Ruth replies, 'I'm in need of company. My husband and his brother have recently died; my sister-in-law has returned home to her family, and my mother-in-law is keeping very tight-lipped, for reasons she is keeping to herself. Since this system has gone live, I've been aching for a little company. I feel so alone, so isolated.'

CyberCindy is bemused at Ruth's confession. She is no bereavement counsellor. She has come here for some fun, not to liase with a suffering avatar.

(Avatar: animated figure.)

? *The Engineer has programmed Ruth with an almost inexhaustible reference system, allowing her to perform her own research and analysis within seconds. She has also been given a personality which will respond with inevitable psychological reactions in certain circumstances.*

And so it is that the technological revolution has finally come of age: an animated screen figure, which in truth is a modem housing a set of electronic pulses and commands – a lifeless box – appears to have thoughts and emotions. Created by humans using their cumulative knowledge over many years, the avatar is almost equal now in communication capabilities to the human.

Ruth's personality has been determined by a team of programmers, who in turn have sought the cumulative wisdom of a number of Old Testament scholars. But does she have the capacity to demonstrate what it means to live by faith? After all, what distinguishes human beings from all other living things is that God has made them in his own image.

'Well, Ruth, honeybun,' CyberCindy responds flippantly, 'I'm glad you're pleased to see me, but let's just get one or two things straight. You are here for my entertainment; I am not here for some sort of personal growth enrichment encounter.' CyberCindy finds being rude quite easy, on a par with being witty.

Ruth blinks at CyberCindy, observing her coolly. CyberCindy assumes she is disappointed, or hurt, and unable to express herself.

'Hey, I didn't mean you any harm. I just want to have fun, that's all, y'know.'

Ruth's lips part gently into an unwilling smile. It is hard for her not to reveal to CyberCindy the seriousness with which she approaches life. Life is much more than an opportunity for fun to her; and yet she sees in CyberCindy a freshness of approach which is appealing and winsome.

'I hope we can have some fun together, too, CyberCindy,' Ruth says, melancholically 'because right at this moment in time I could do with someone to make me laugh.' Ruth smiles her gentle smile again, and

CyberCindy feels oddly disempowered. She has rarely had such a conversation revealing so much vulnerability with anyone in so short a time of meeting.

The women continue walking, and CyberCindy takes the opportunity to scan the scenery about her. Her main impression is one of harshness. The earth beneath her feet is dusty and stony, hard and unyielding. The path they are walking on is loosely determined by a sweep of stones, almost rubble, white and irregular. Olive trees and spiny bushes give relief to the general landscape of dusty earth; in the distance, though, CyberCindy can see fields on the hillside.

After a while, they come to a single house by the side of the road; outside is a goat, which is attached to a post by a large thick rope. A man is sitting on a stool, his head leaning back on the front wall, catching the shade created by a sheet hanging down from the flat roof, his scrawny face a jigsaw of wrinkles. His eyes are shut, and he appears to be asleep. As he hears the women approach, however, the man quickly rises from his seat, motioning at them to stop and take a rest inside the house.

A large woman comes out of the house, her hands white with flour; and seeing the visitors she does a quick U-turn through the front doorway, returning with three large clay mugs and a jug of water. The man and woman talk rapidly to the women; CyberCindy has no idea what they are saying, for they are speaking a foreign language.

The man suddenly gesticulates to CyberCindy, offering her the water. Her throat feels sticky and woolly; she would like to drink. She declines his offer, but subsequently puts the scene on hold, and pressing a button on her SceneSensa, returns for a moment to her apartment. The mug of coffee is still on her desk. She takes a couple of enthusiastic gulps, almost spilling the coffee as she does so, for she is slightly disorientated.

Having satisfied her thirst, CyberCindy quickly returns to the virtual world of Ruth, where the couple are jabbering on somewhat emphatically to Ruth and the other woman, whom CyberCindy has assumed is Naomi. They decline the offer of hospitality; they move on again, the pace slightly quicker than before, after the donkeys have had a drink at the water trough by the side of the house.

Ruth turns to CyberCindy with quiet determination.

'For two or three thousand years, CyberCindy, my story has been summarised as a tale of charm and delight. Goethe called it "the loveliest complete work on a small scale, handed down to us as an ethical treatise and an idyll". And someone else said that, "no poet in the world has written a more beautiful short story".[33] She pauses for a moment, possibly to analyse CyberCindy's reaction, but CyberCindy says nothing and she continues, 'That may or may not be so, but there is more to me than the beauty of words.'

CyberCindy surmises that Ruth has a chip on her shoulder to start talking like this; but she appreciates her frankness and, as is common in cyberspace, answers rather brusquely.

'I don't really know what you're going on about, Ruth. I just enjoyed your story, and thought it would be fun to meet you.'

? *Hedonism, the pursuit of pleasure, is a major aspect of postmodernity. Whilst this is perceived as being 'anti-Christian', the irony is that celebration is at the heart of authentic Christianity. Christ gives abundant life (John 10:10);*

> *a life lived in awe of God is a life lived in worshipful celebration of his love. Heaven is portrayed as a great banquet in one of Jesus' parables (Luke 14:15–35); joy is fundamental to living in relationship with God (Philippians 4:4). It is the joy of being in relationship with God, and the hope for the future which that brings, which empowers believers to confront godlessness.*

'I am glad you enjoyed reading my story, CyberCindy,' Ruth responds rather doggedly, 'Many people have spent a great deal of time studying me.'

CyberCindy fears she has bitten off more than she can chew. She thinks Ruth rather absurd and arrogant, but then remembers she has recently been bereaved and so may not be behaving rationally.

'Oh, really,' CyberCindy is not sure how to respond and is not particularly impressed. She is inclined to be anti-intellectual, preferring experience to theory. She feels she wants a bit of time to assimilate her experience, but takes Ruth's bait in any case, 'Studying you?'

'Yes. Some folk think that my book is about the liberation of God's people from the land of oppression and death and the re-seeding of them and their land.'[34]

> ❜ Whether it is women, land or ideas, the normal male mode of relationship is one of conquer or be conquered, dominate or be dominated.[35]

Some argue that the central theme is kindness,' she smiles assuredly, 'but most scholars are agreed that the central focus is providence,' Ruth pauses, 'and I agree with them too … up to a point.'

CyberCindy interrupts, 'What's providence?', she asks impatiently. She is affronted at Ruth's assumption of her understanding. She has never heard the term 'God's people' before, and the talk about reseeding goes way above her head.

'Providence?', Ruth repeats the question, 'Providence is all about God's care and protection of the world after its creation, so that it moves forward in a line towards a specific goal. You can see this as my narrative progresses to the steady resolution of Naomi's complaint.'[36]

'Naomi's complaint?', CyberCindy wonders if Naomi had arthritis or some other similar ailment. She decides not to interrupt again, but determines to see if there is a FAQ on Ruth once she gets out of virtual reality.

(FAQ: Frequently Asked Questions, a document found in most Usenet groups, with questions [and answers] that are most commonly asked by newcomers to the group.)

CyberCindy returns her attention to what Ruth is saying. 'Others believe my book is directed against restrictions on intermarriage.'

'Restrictions on intermarriage?', the words have no meaning to CyberCindy, who has no respect for restrictions and no understanding of what intermarriage is. She is just about to interrupt Ruth again, but Ruth is following her own agenda, and seems determined to divulge copious learned information and educate CyberCindy on matters concerning herself.

'I have also been heralded as a model for proselytes likening my acceptance of God to one symbolising Israel's acceptance to the Torah. Others suggest that my story is an ancestral one concerning the great King David, because it ends with a genealogy.'[37]

(Proselyte: a non-Jew who fully participated in Jewish religion.)

(Torah: the Law of Moses/first five books of the Bible, also known as the Pentateuch.)

After her explanation, Ruth pauses to take a stone out of her sandal. She has been quite animated, and behind her thoughtful assessment of the various scholars that had studied her story exudes an excitement which pervades the space between her and CyberCindy, and somehow seems to demand attention. In spite of her reservations, CyberCindy feels constrained to listen to her. CyberCindy is not feeling quite so comfortable now, for strangely she does not feel fully in command of her situation even though she knows she is in charge of all the controls. The slight unease she experienced on arrival is beginning to germinate within her again; but for the time being, because she is not sure quite what is happening, she decides to stick with it. Ruth is using academic parlance that CyberCindy finds distasteful. But she likes adventure, after all, and is really quite excited to be talking with Ruth, the heroine of the story.

As the three women continue their walk, CyberCindy glances past Ruth to the other woman accompanying them: Naomi. Her features are strong, although time has taken its toll and her skin is dark, cracked and lined. There is an air of monotony about the woman, dressed entirely in black, like Ruth. Just looking at her depresses CyberCindy. Naomi looks only ahead, her eyes resolutely fixed on the road before them, not moving to the left or right. The older woman advances steadily, doggedly, her walk slow but sure, and her hands which are large and bony, grasp the donkey's bridle firmly. CyberCindy notices that Naomi's lips are tight and pursed, and every so often the woman chews on her lower lip.

CyberCindy tries to engage her in conversation, 'You must be Naomi,' she says. But Naomi does not respond at all. It seems that she is not contactable. A glance to her user-sensor indicates that there is only one other user present, and that, CyberCindy concludes erroneously, must be Ruth.

Without prompting, Ruth continues her philosophical assessment. 'I appreciate that any biblical narrative will be idealised to some extent, but I would like you, CyberCindy, to ask questions of me that have not been asked before. I would like you to inhabit my world, but with the experience and questions which your world asks, and so illuminate the text and even challenge previous understandings. I would like you, CyberCindy, to find what relevance my story has for people living in your world. I want to show you that although we are separated by two horizons, God's word is timeless. When my story is reduced to one only of charm and delight, its theological significance is in danger of being overlooked.' She pauses, as if she is weighing up whether she should continue. She makes her decision,

'What is more, I have been interpreted largely from a male perspective. Whilst women have contributed many short articles, it is the men who have supplied detailed analysis in the form of Biblical commentaries.[38] Many of the male insights have been profound. But I would like you to interpret me from a female perspective, to see if the conclusions you draw agree with the vast majority of scholars.'

Ruth pauses to draw breath.

Naomi plods on determinedly, taking no interest whatsoever in Ruth's little speech. 'You see, my story is quite special for its day because women, not men, occupy central stage.[39] This is rather unusual in a patriarchal society. But I think I have something to say, quite apart from the virtues of loyalty and love, don't you?'

> 9 The only way to eliminate the fascism in our heads is to explore and build upon the open qualities of human discourse.[40]

'Oh dear,' CyberCindy responds, 'No, I don't, not at the moment anyway. I'm not sure I can give you a female perspective, or any perspective at all. I'm not sure I can be bothered with you, Ruth. You're rather irrelevant to me, you see. To tell you the truth, it was the love story bit that I found appealing.'

Ruth's whole demeanour seems to change as CyberCindy speaks. She is clearly insulted. But CyberCindy is unperturbed.

orange

'Ruth, you can't dictate the questions I will ask of you. You can't put me into a box and expect me to conform. I don't think I can look at you from a female perspective. On the Internet I prefer being androgynous. I don't like stereotyping.'

? *The Internet offers punters the opportunity to become 'transgenders', that is to create their own identities, myths and histories. Postmodernity is polymorphous or androgenous; it rejects stable boundaries, which are interpreted as being mechanisms for control. The traditional male/female role models are superseded and a complex web of male/female traits is embraced. However, whilst androgyny or polymorphism may be one of postmodernity's ideals (in that androgyny is truly relative), it cannot be the actual. People are born male or female, and can escape the limitations of their bodies only by turning to medical adaptation. To dismiss sexual differences is to deny actuality, but worse than that it evades the injustices which patriarchal cultures essentially promote. Postmodern culture is still dominated by men. Whilst the subordination of women is politically incorrect and ethically uncomfortable, 'it can expect no particular relief by appeal to postmodernity'.[41]*

Ruth turns to CyberCindy and responds icily, 'If you knew me a little better, you would know that I don't like stereotyping either, CyberCindy.' There is firmness in her voice, which makes CyberCindy cringe because she has an inbuilt prejudice against all authority. But then Ruth takes her by surprise and asks, 'But, tell me, what do you mean by postmodern?'

CyberCindy feels a sense of relief. At last, the all-knowing Ruth has acknowledged that she doesn't know everything. CyberCindy hadn't realised how tense she had become listening to Ruth's didactic way of speaking. She recognises that she has been on the defensive. Ruth's sudden admission of ignorance makes her feel as though she has something to contribute after all.

'Oh, well, uh ...' CyberCindy struggles to put together a coherent explanation. 'I used to think it just meant after-modern, you know like post-natal (after-birth) or post-script (after-writing) ... but then I saw the end of a weird documentary-type programme on the telly the other day.'

Ruth is bemused.

'They say it's as radical as the Enlightenment was and that we're heading for a sort of revolutionary new social order, except order's the wrong word.' CyberCindy is struggling to be coherent. She doesn't find it easy.

'The Enlightenment?', Ruth queries, for she naturally gravitates towards words that convey something of knowledge and revelation.

'Yeah', CyberCindy gathers speed. She hasn't spoken like this to anyone in a long time. 'The emphasis on reason, y'know, and intellectualism and the belief in progress, that somehow we are achieving things and getting better.

Nobody believes that any more. We're not going anywhere, we simply are. Each age has its achievements and accomplishments. But we're not progressing, not in a true sense. We think we're so clever these days with all our mod cons, but y'know, the Romans had central heating long before us.'

'Central heating?', Ruth appears to be perplexed. CyberCindy smirks. 'Where I come from,' she explains with an air of superiority, 'we only get sunshine about a third of the year!'

Ruth blinks dispassionately again. CyberCindy wonders if Ruth believes her. She is quietly pleased to discover that she knows something that Ruth doesn't. She takes this opportunity, having found a willing audience, to express her philosophy on life in general.

'Ruth, you do know, don't you, that there isn't any central purpose to life? We live, we die, we laugh, we cry. That's it. And there certainly isn't any such thing as objective truth. Truth claims are just about little people clutching at opportunities to make themselves big. You do know, don't you Ruth, that the church only propagates religion to maintain power?'

Ruth digests CyberCindy's analysis and then responds gently, 'But CyberCindy, you can't dismiss reality just like that. Surely, if life is to have meaning, something has to be true? Truth has to exist.'

CyberCindy's worse fears and suspicions are realised. Ruth is a fundamentalist.

'Look,' she says aggressively, 'you asked me what postmodernity was. Do you really want to know, or do you just want to stay stuck in your own little time warp, not learning anything? Do you really care where I'm coming from, or do you just want to indoctrinate me with irrelevant clichés ?'

Ruth blushes with the pain of knowing she has been misunderstood. 'Sorry. Please continue.'

CyberCindy doesn't want to continue. She doesn't want to waste her time talking to Ruth, for she perceives a dogma in her which is distasteful and unappealing. She hesitates, having taken umbrage at Ruth's stance. Ruth senses CyberCindy's hesitation. 'Please?', she prompts.

CyberCindy decides to be forgiving, and taking a deep breath, continues to explain the little she knows concerning postmodernity.

'Modernity promoted capitalism, industrialisation, urbanisation and democracy. Some people think that postmodern just means after-modern, the next stage after modernity. But that's not quite what it is. Postmodernity is all about questioning modernity, because modernity hasn't come up with the promised goods. But what we know can't save us. What we know isn't enough, is it? This age isn't better than the last one, or the one before that, it's just different. We're not getting any better, we just know more, or different things, that's all. And the more we know doesn't help. Look at the achievements of the twentieth century – racism, sexism, pollution, war, and AIDS. We're destroying the rain forests, the ozone layer; we're destroying one another … since the enlightenment people have assumed that they are in control. But look at the Titanic – the unsinkable ship – the great symbol of technological advancement. People thought they could conquer the waves. What a joke! Everyone who went on that ship thought it was unsinkable; the orchestra even continued to play as the ship went down, they all believed the lie that had been sold to them, until, of course, most of them drowned. Nobody believes we're getting better any more. Look at the crime rates for a start. We're just on a road to nowhere.'

Ruth was disturbed now, not so much by the facts, which she knew anyway, but with CyberCindy's cynicism.

'Well, if you really believe the human race is going nowhere,' she responds, 'why are you spending time talking to me?'

This time it is CyberCindy who smiles.

'You help kill time. And besides, you're past history,' she replies with an air of arrogance.

They walk on together in silence whilst Ruth grasps the implications of what CyberCindy is saying.

Eventually, Ruth says, 'Well, my time is precious. So don't come here accessing me if you don't really want to know what I'm about. You just block up the system and mess up other people's chances of discovering truth.'

> **?** *One of the most effective ways to engage with the Bible is to allow the text to give its own answers, being aware of our own assumptions as we read it.*

CyberCindy realises that Ruth is honest and direct and not to be messed about with.

She decides that talking to her beats reading *boING boING.*[42]

'OK then, I'll try to listen to you, and I'll try to understand you, so long as you try to understand me too and don't try to indoctrinate me with all your bigoted perceptions.'

'Fine,' Ruth answers wisely, unperturbed by CyberCindy's assessment of her motives.

yellow

The three women continue on their journey to Bethlehem. Naomi remains silent, but Ruth is keen to talk.

'CyberCindy, it occurs to me that you and I have more in common than you perhaps realise, and that the dawn of the twenty-first century is a particularly appropriate time for you to read me.'

'Why?', asks CyberCindy, curiously cautious.

> *Some parts of the Bible are more obviously relevant to certain times and situations than other parts. This is not to relativise God's word, rather it is to claim that God has accommodated for our needs through his revelation by his provision of a variety of genres throughout the Scriptures. Surprisingly, Ruth, a book renowned for its gentle beauty, may be especially relevant for those living on the cusp of the twenty-first century, but not necessarily for traditional reasons.*

'Well, the book of Ruth is set in the days when the judges ruled. "In those days Israel had no king; everyone did as he saw fit."[43] These are heady days of battle and conquest, with no certainties, and where individuals have to discover and establish their own boundaries – social, political and religious. The people of Israel are forging foundations for generations to come, but they are also living in a time of flux and turmoil … and of godlessness.' Ruth pauses to flick a fly away from her face, 'That's not so different from the society that you're living in now, is it?'

CyberCindy reacts immediately, 'I think that's rather a sweeping generalisation. I don't deny that within postmodernity there is chaos. But postmodernity is not forging foundations. With the death of modernity we have to accept that there are now no foundations at all. This is what you need to understand. There is no security except in there being no security. If that is what godlessness is, then I suppose there is a similarity. But postmodernity has erupted like a volcano from the mists of modernity; it smashes all previous assumptions and conceptions and it questions every previously accepted ideology. Is that what the time of the judges was like? I don't think it is possible for one age to be like another. All is dissimilarity.'

Ruth disagrees, 'Perhaps, but there is similarity in that "everyone does as they see fit". People rely on their own perceptions, rather than on the perceptions which God has revealed to them through his mighty, saving acts.'

CyberCindy is silent. She has no comprehension of what God's mighty, saving acts might be. She finds Ruth's language rather odd. Ruth continues, 'Anyway, if you won't accept that, you may like to remember that I am in mourning, which is, I think where postmodernity is at, just now. I have lost my old way of life. You have lost modernity. I have lost my security. You don't have any. Yet I have hope. Listen to me and perhaps you, too, will find hope.'

? *An element of failure has always been present within modernity – hence theories of alienation (Marx), anomie (Durkheim), the homeless mind (Berger) and the iron cage (Weber). And modern science has always been open to abuse and misuse. But today it seems that great achievements have turned sour. The atomic bomb maims and destroys; X-rays cause cancer; cars cause pollution. The resulting disenchantment seeks love and tolerance, but it cannot trust, for it is disillusioned. Claiming that there are no absolutes does involve pain, for it leads to insecurity and undermines any claims of certain knowledge. If there are no absolutes, then everything is theory, everything is subject to interpretation, and everything is open to discussion. Life becomes surreal.*

Kubler Ross has identified denial, isolation, anger, bargaining, depression, acceptance and hope as specific reactions to mourning. Interestingly, with the exception of hope, all these elements are components of postmodernity.[44] *Is society truly grieving for modernity, resplendent in its arrogant certainty? Perhaps it is, but the grieving will not resurrect the past. Whilst death brings unavoidable loss it also paves the way for new discovery. We are living in exciting times.*

CyberCindy isn't quite sure that she understands death. She can't decide whether it is the final ultimate experience of life, or simply a change of frequency, a moving over into another dimension. As for mourning, postmodernity brings escape and release for her, and the opportunity to engage in endless philosophy. She turns to Ruth.

'I thought I was supposed to be the one with the ideas?', CyberCindy accuses pointedly. Ruth says no more.

violet

CyberCindy is suddenly hot and feels rather claustrophobic. She switches the knob on her visor, and looks about for her coffee cup again. She takes a large swig, 'Ughh! It's cold!' However, the drink refreshes her, and she flips back the visor to continue her conversation with Ruth. The brief pause in the encounter has caused CyberCindy to recognise that she is getting a real buzz out of her discussion with this virtual Ruth.

They walk on together for a time. CyberCindy wonders at the expanse around her; undulating slopes with hills and mountains in the distance, none of which throw up very much greenery. The land has been ravaged by the heat and appears lifeless and dry.

Ruth again takes the initiative in the discussion and asks, 'Why did you choose me?'

CyberCindy replies honestly, 'I just thought I would suss out a few religions and see which one most appealed to me.'

'But why me?', Ruth persists.

'Chance,' CyberCindy pauses, 'Pure chance.'

Ruth is apparently dissatisfied with this answer, and perseveres with her questioning, 'Do you think I've got anything to offer you?'

'Possibly,' (defensively), 'but I suppose, really, I just like a story. I'm not into big answers or big stories, but the little story of Ruth somehow got to me … little people and their little lives, a personal story about one particular family...it starts off sad and it ends happily ... and it is full of irony. And I like irony!'

Ruth nods, 'Yes, you are right about the irony. The story begins in Bethlehem, which means "House of Bread", where there is no bread, because there is famine. Elimelech and his family go to Moab, (the place where the Israelites found no food when they were on their wanderings through the desert to find food).[45] Elimelech leaves Bethlehem in pursuit of life, but he and his sons find death. Naomi claims she left Bethlehem full, when she was literally hungry, and that she has returned empty, when she had been fed, although the stated motivation for her return was that there was food again in Bethlehem. She left Bethlehem full because she had two Israelite sons, but she leaves Moab empty because she has one foreign daughter-in-law. Not only that, Naomi can't provide for her daughter-in-laws, but also I provide a son for Naomi. Boaz is described as a man of standing, and yet from the genealogy in Matthew 1:5 we learn that he was the son of Rahab the prostitute. And of course the names in the story are all rather significant to their characters, rather like your name, CyberCindy, tells us something about you.[46]

CyberCindy is flattered. She wonders what it is Ruth thinks her name conveys. She hopes it is something sexy.

My part in the narrative is as a barren female, a widow, and a Moabite – the cursed race which was a result of Lot's incest with his daughter. So I am a foreigner and the lowest of the low in Israelite eyes, but I finish as great grandmother to King David, forerunner to the Messiah, the Holy and Anointed One. When I echo Boaz's words of blessing to me when I am with him on the threshing floor that really is overflowing with irony, don't you think?

Perhaps the greatest irony of all, however, is that Boaz is presented as the key illustration of the kinsman redeemer.'

> **?** *The Kinsman-Redeemer (see Leviticus 25:25–27, 47–49) arose because the Israelites held three things dear to their hearts: family; keeping family land in the family; and having descendants. In Hebrew the word go'el means Kinsman-Redeemer. If a man sold a piece of his property or land through poverty, a brother or other near relation was expected, out of family loyalty, to go and buy back or 'redeem' that land and give it back to the impoverished relatives. This, if it was implemented, gave a strong commitment of protection and care towards one's family members.*

'Of course Boaz is this, but it is me who redeems the whole situation outlined in the story, for I not only redeem Naomi from her physical destitution and psychological trauma, I redeem Boaz from his dilemma as to how to fulfil his obligations, and ultimately I am the pivotal means by which Yahweh chooses to redeem his people Israel. Without a Ruth, there would not have been a David. Without a David there would have been no hope of a Messiah.'

> **"** The exploration of contradictions always lies at the heart of original thought. [47]

> **?** *Although the text constantly calls Ruth 'Ruth the Moabite', her significance as a woman and a foreigner is generally lost to modern readers because of her commitment to Yahweh. In order to really come to terms with Ruth's strategic role and Naomi's condition, we need to recognize the social*

stigma which ancient Israel attached to women unable to marry and bear children. The Moabites were cursed, not simply foreigners. The radical nature of the Book of Ruth must not be overlooked: Ruth was initially a nobody in the society she sought to adopt. The mention of David in 4:17 has been thought to provide the full interpretative framework for the book of Ruth. But given that the ancient reader would know from the beginning how the story would end, we can still ask why David's ancestors should be of any importance. Could it be that early on in salvation history, God was making a statement which has not been properly investigated: that he chose an isolated, foreign woman to redeem his chosen people Israel? Some suggest that Obed is the true redeemer – a baby, a voiceless minor. But Obed is the product of redemption; he is the culmination of Ruth's saving acts, not the genesis of them.

Male preconceptions of female roles may have fogged a simple analysis of the story, for redemption is undoubtedly the primary focus of the book of Ruth. Whilst providence may be an important thread, the redemption of Ruth and Naomi, and subsequently the redemption of all Israel is quite clearly the central issue; it begs no special pleading, no clever interpretation.

CyberCindy says nothing in response to Ruth's analysis. She can see that Ruth feels passionately about her part in history, in fact about her part in the canon of Scripture.

(Canon of Scripture: what the Christian church has decreed and accepted as constituting God's revelation to people; namely the Bible.)

All this talk of redemption means nothing to her. Ruth continues her dialogue, which is turning into something of a monologue, 'Typologically, too, there may be significance in my narrative, in that there is the birth of a baby boy who brings joy, there is a *go'el* who redeems, and in the ambiguous threshing floor scene, when I ask Boaz to spread the corner of his garment over me, this could be a foretaste of the Holy Spirit overshadowing Mary.[48] I could argue that the whole book of Ruth looks towards the New Testament for a fuller interpretation. But these are just passing thoughts; I may be trying too hard to make myself more important than I have already been made. But do you see that to establish my story as only a charming narrative of love, idealising me as the perfect female role-model, is to do me something of a disservice? God put me in the Scriptures for a reason, and I don't think it was simply to give the world a poetic love story. After all, I am heralded as being worth more than seven sons!'

(Typology: study and interpretation of general types.)

CyberCindy doesn't understand the value of sons or typology, and she doesn't wish to. She looks up and realises that they have been approaching a town, comprised of small white houses, capped with flat roofs. She realises that they have reached Bethlehem.

'Is there anywhere we can get a pizza in this place?', she asks, for the talk of Naomi's fullness and emptiness has made CyberCindy feel physically hungry.

Sometimes, when CyberCindy is working, she can order a pizza or a sandwich in her virtual working office, and get it delivered to her real-life door.

She is disappointed to learn that the creators of the virtual world of Ruth have not accommodated for her physical needs: she surmises that she must be in a very new venture, a very new world. She suddenly feels frustrated and uncomfortable, and because Ruth answers her question negatively, CyberCindy decides, rather impetuously, to exit Ruth, which she does without saying goodbye.

? *CyberCindy's spiritual quest to find meaning, truth and knowledge, is on a par with consuming mass produced food, which is always available. She finds it hard to conceive of seasonal variations and harder still to imagine or dwell on famine and its implications.*

CyberCindy has always found her identity in consumerism, she finds meaning in the very act of consuming. 'I shop, therefore I am.' Keith Tester has described postmodernism using a shopping mall metaphor where the individual is there to have fun and where the people are seduced, and offered the right to 'thoroughly individual' choice.[49] *Ironically, however, social approval is required for the choice, and this is what the shopping mall gives.*

The shopping mall, the new cathedral of society, houses those who have come to worship the god of materialism and delight in finding their identity in things purchased. But ironically the shopping mall also houses those whose function it is to work in the shops. They are constrained by their work contracts; enclosed environment; and rules of social order and etiquette. Meanwhile the consumer is at liberty to wander where he or she will; she can go hither and thither from this shop to that, worshipping the god of want; and because s/he has money in her pocket, s/he has a form of power, which is non-dependent on status. He or she can buy what he or she likes, when he or she likes. The shop worker, meanwhile, is bound by rules and restrictions.

Similarly, modernity's prime concern (like that of the shop assistant) is production and service; whilst postmodernity is consumed with consumption. Thus postmodernity and modernity are intertwined in an inextricable relationship, the one dependent upon the other for survival. It simply isn't fair that modernity has to work, whilst postmodernity plays. Modernity knows that if it plays it will die. By contrast, youthful postmodernity is unwilling to accept any responsibility – everyone has a right to play, don't they?

Postmodernity may bring liberation but if postmodern thought is taken to its logical conclusion there would be no dialogue at all. Whilst CyberCindy may believe herself to be a liberated postmodern, elements of modernity are still (necessarily) present in her thinking, much to her own annoyance. Postmodern thinking is dependant upon modern philosophy for its status; like a leech it will suck the life-blood from modernity; like a toddler it will spit it out. But what is modernity's life-blood? Control, order, stability? Progression, suppression, obsession?

On her way home CyberCindy stops at Gibson to order a pizza. Whilst she is there she scans the Web Directory to see if any other biblical virtual worlds exist. She rather fancies dipping into the time of the Judges, and witnessing some of their barbarism, but she is disappointed to discover that there is no virtual world for the book of Judges. She also discovers that Ruth is one of the first Old Testament books to have been developed, and that the virtual reality Ruth is a prototype, an experiment. She wonders who has put the whole thing together, who is pulling the strings. Usually, virtual worlds are widely advertised long before they go live, and so are their makers. The entry beside Ruth on the Web Directory of Worlds, under Company, is 'Name & Address Supplied on Application'. CyberCindy is annoyed: why would the web maker withhold their name, were they ashamed of their product? CyberCindy also sees an advert for the New Testament Gospels.

'Coming Soon!', it announces, 'Matthew, Mark, Luke and John – enter the world of Christ on earth, meet the people he met, go where he went, see him perform signs, miracles and wonders.' A large conglomerate called Highway was developing the Gospels. This discovery causes CyberCindy some considerable excitement. She isn't ready to meet Jesus just yet, she surmises. But as she swims the rest of her journey home, the thought of an encounter with him amuses her as she anticipates various scenarios.

Once home, CyberCindy strips off her Grips and her SceneSensa. She unplugs her Rompacomp, and closes down her machine. She runs her hands through her short blonde hair instinctively, now that she has the freedom to do so, and as she glances around her eyes halt on the clock. It is 15:45 hrs. She has missed her appointment at the gym. She awaits the delivery of her pizza, and when it arrives chomps through the food lustily, hardly pausing between mouthfuls.

green

Carl calls by in the evening, bringing a video and a few
cans with him. They munch crisps and swig beer,
watching the video – a surreal comedy – until Carl's
bleeper goes off, and he is gone, leaving CyberCindy with
two cans of lager and a half empty packet of crisps for
company.

That night as she lies on her bed in her small, isolated
apartment, CyberCindy ponders on her meanderings in
cyberspace. There was something about Ruth that was
incredibly attractive, and it wasn't her looks. It was her
integrity.

> **?** *There was a rabbinic tradition that Ruth was a
> physically beautiful woman. But it is Ruth's
> character, rather than her looks, which Boaz
> found appealing. In contrast to the postmodern
> emphasis on the visual, Ruth challenges appeal to
> illusion with an appeal to the actual. Being real is
> costly, and Ruth is prepared to pay the cost through
> the way she lives her life.*

Before going to sleep, CyberCindy remembers that in the
corner of the loft there is a pile of old books, left there by
a previous owner. She is pretty sure that one of them is a
Bible. She gets out of bed, puts on her dressing gown,
and pulls down the loft ladder, 'Maybe I'm mad,' she
mutters to herself as she climbs the ladder and opens the
loft door. It is very cold and black. She turns on the light

and momentarily flinches. The floor is dusty and the air
is still. There is an old mirror lying on its side;
CyberCindy catches her reflection in it with disdain – she
looks a mess. But there in the corner, just as she
remembered, are the books. She crawls over to them and
picks up the top one, blowing the dust off the cover.
Institutes of the Christian Religion, Volume I, by John
Calvin. She puts it to one side, a tremulous excitement
stirring within her. She picks up the next book, *Institutes
of the Christian Religion, Volume II*, by John Calvin. She
wonders what an institute of religion might be, and then
her eye catches what she had been looking for, there,
second up from the bottom, is the Bible she was hoping
to find. She pulls it out from the pile, and the books on
top of it fall to the floor with a loud thump. She holds it
in her hands and smiles. It is red and rather tatty. On its
front, in gold, is written *Good News Bible. Illustrated.*
'Good,' she thought, 'I like pictures.'

Then she scrambles along the dusty floor once more,
turning off the light as she descends the loft ladder. Her
dressing gown is covered with dust, which she smacks off
before hanging it up on the back of the door. Then she
gets into bed and leafs through the pages rapidly, their
flimsy thinness giving a pleasing feel to the pages laden
with words, simple pencil sketches giving light relief here
and there. She finds what she is looking for, and begins to
read. There is a part of her psyche that can't quite believe
she is doing this; there is another part which is thriving
on it. She reads well into the night, and wakes up in the
morning with the *Good News Bible* sharing her pillow.

The next day CyberCindy feels compelled to meet Ruth
in virtual reality once more. Besides which, she has very
little else to do. Work is going smoothly at the moment.

She has a few meetings in cyberspace coming up and is aware that she will have to address a suspicion she has that someone has been cribbing her ideas whilst she has been on conference call; but all that can wait. She went to sleep thinking about her encounter with Ruth, and she wakes up thinking about it.

Whilst in the shower, she vaguely registers that she ought to empty the bin and catch up on some exercise, but after drying herself she, instinctively – almost recklessly – reaches for her Rompacomp and makes for the machinery on her desk. She willingly goes through the same rigmarole as she did the previous day, carefully easing herself into the Rompacomp, stroking her legs and arms firmly to ensure a full and satisfactory sensation experience. This time rather than flying, CyberCindy chooses the tube as her mode of transport. It has been a long time since she has experienced the jostling, the silent stares, the ching, ching, ching of someone's Walkman and the rhythmic swaying of the train. Despite the dullness on people's faces, and being squashed by a large fellow sitting on her left, she enjoys the trip enormously, and resolves to travel by tube again, soon. The train pulls up at a station, and CyberCindy sees the same gate she saw yesterday. She leaves her seat and alights from the train, approaching the gate with some anticipation. She has something to ask Ruth.

On entry, she is aware once more of being alone, on a solitary journey. She feels a mixture of emotions – excitement and apprehension.

As CyberCindy approaches the two women, plodding on, all in black, Ruth turns around and greets CyberCindy with a warm but rather enigmatic smile. CyberCindy goes directly to the point.

'There's something I need to ask you, Ruth.'

'Please go ahead,' Ruth smiles.

? *Whilst the virtual world of Ruth can be entered as many times as desired, and at any point in the narrative, Ruth the avatar has been designed to memorise and recall every encounter she has with each cyber traveller. In this way, she can build up a relationship with those who encounter her in cyberspace, easily recalling the last time they met and their conversation. Human beings, on the other hand, do not have such reliable memory chips.*

'What made you pledge yourself to Naomi? Why didn't you just go home?'

Ruth smiles again, this time largely to herself, pleased that CyberCindy is keen to delve more deeply into her story.

'There was no point in me going home. Nobody would want to marry me, a barren widow of a foreign man. And I would only be a burden to my family, or else a skivvy for my brothers' wives. But Naomi's prospects were worse than mine, for Elimelech's estate will be inherited by the nearest living male. She is either menopausal or has gone through the menopause, so she can't produce babies, which means she has now lost all claim to any inheritance.'

? *Ruth 1:12 indicates that Naomi is past childbearing age. The death of both her sons, following Elimelech's death, has brought Naomi unexpected destitution because the family line has come to an end. There were no provisions* *enabling the widow to inherit the property of her deceased husband in those times, and the nearest kinsman of the husband would have succeeded to the estate. The law of levirate marriage ensured the continuation of the family line and also protected the widow. However, it may have been rarely implemented because fathering a child on behalf of a deceased man meant that inheritance rights, which would otherwise naturally go to the nearest living male (the kinsman redeemer), would be given to the new son. It was therefore not in the material interests of the surviving male to facilitate the loss of his inheritance.*

'She has no future, and no hope. Yet there was a real godliness within Naomi. Some people paint a picture of a selfish Naomi, making me out to be especially godly in contrast. But she wasn't selfish. That's why she told Orpah and me to go back to our families. She didn't want to be a burden to us. She seemed to depend on her God in a way that I didn't understand, and Mahlon too, was much more caring of me than most Moabite men would have been. I regarded myself as Naomi's daughter. I loved her. I couldn't leave her to face the journey to Bethlehem on her own, or to arrive there not knowing what hardships lay before her. And I knew I had to commit myself to Yahweh if I was going to accompany Naomi to Bethlehem. All her people served this God. I couldn't return with her and still worship my own gods. That would cause Naomi even more embarrassment to add to her humiliation of returning with no husband and no sons.'

CyberCindy is intrigued, 'So, you chose Yahweh for convenience, then?'

'Don't be superficial, CyberCindy,' Ruth responds, 'I chose Yahweh because I was joining Yahweh's community. If I was going to commit myself to Naomi, I had to commit myself to her God. Her situation was desolate. Elimelech may have been fairly wealthy, someone who had standing in the community. As his wife, and as bearer of his sons, she had a certain standing, a status within the community. But famine is no respecter of status ... turning your back on your community in order to find food is a fairly desperate measure. Naomi's return is humiliating for her, especially as she regards her circumstances as evidently being God's judgement upon her. But that didn't stop her from wanting to bless Orpah and me. She still prays that her God will look after us. And she accepts that everything that has happened has been orchestrated by God, that she and we are in his hands. This is what I call faith. Naomi's relationship with God was real. She doesn't reject him because awful things happen to her. Her God was manifestly a part of her life. I couldn't pledge myself to her and her people and keep my own gods. It wouldn't have worked; it would have been keeping my distance. I think that was why she was fearful of us accompanying her. We simply would not have been integrated into her society if we had kept our gods.' After a brief pause Ruth persevered, 'I think that people would fare a little better in the world if they were to take responsibility for their own actions.'

> *Ruth is fully prepared to take responsibility for her own actions in the world, and it is this aspect of her character that catapults her into the role of redeemer. Ruth's confession in 1:16–17 reveals a loyalty and commitment which will be borne out in the rest of the text, and which results in God's blessing. Ruth is a model for both male and female believers. However, because self-sacrifice is perceived as a natural element of a woman's character and role, it is usually expected, and even demanded, of her. If Ruth and Naomi had been men, one wonders what lessons would have been pulled out of the text. Ruth's loyalty to another individual in times of hardship, with no obvious benefit to herself, is a challenge to the postmodern emphasis on hedonism – if it feels good, do it.*

'You sound rather arrogant and intolerant to me, Ruth. I don't think that's very godly,' CyberCindy retorted.

'But I'm not intolerant of good,' Ruth replies defensively, 'I'm intolerant of bad.'

CyberCindy scoffed, 'Who are you to say what is good and what is bad?' She is offended at Ruth's claim to moral discernment, 'What's good for you may be bad for someone else.'

> *Commitment to justice is a prime motivating factor in Ruth's actions. But the very concept of justice is rationally incoherent to the fully postmodern individual. CyberCindy hasn't yet grappled with the idea that to affirm one thing might be to deny something else.*

'I wanted to join Naomi's people, because the God of the Israelites, although transcendent, also intervened in the lives of his people, he was real. Through his commandments, through his creation – supremely through the salvation the Israelites found through the exodus – Yahweh had revealed himself to be the Almighty God, faithful to his people. And his people lived in community with one another, in relationship with one another.'

'I suppose that's why he brought Naomi to such a pitiful state, and why the three men in her life died, away from their community?' There was sarcasm in CyberCindy's voice.

? *The reasons for Elimelech's death and the death of his sons are unknown. If their deaths were proof of God's anger following their marriage to Moabite women, why didn't Boaz suffer the same fate? Was it because Ruth, by this stage, had renounced her Moabite roots and embraced Yahweh? Perhaps Boaz, who (unlike the nearest kinsman-redeemer), was prepared to marry a Moabite, was putting into practice the principle of mercy, whereas Elimelech's sons may have married for self-preservation – in order to gain access to land in Moab (paid as a dowry), land which they could farm. Alternatively, they could have died due to war, illness or even starvation.*

'You said yourself, CyberCindy, that the story has a happy ending. We must be patient. And death is in general one of the few certainties of life.'

After a time of quiet, where CyberCindy gazes again at the barren beauty of the scenery around her, she asks another question that had kept her awake the previous night (being a product of her age), 'But what was wrong with your gods?'

> *We know little of the roles and rites associated with ancient gods. The principle god of the Moabites was Chemosh and language used when referring to this god was apparently very similar to the language adopted when speaking of Yahweh. However, other gods were worshipped alongside Chemosh by the Moabites. Naomi refers to Orpah's gods in Ruth 1:15. The distinctiveness of the Israelites was that they were monotheistic. Whilst the Old Testament is littered with references to the Israelites worshipping other gods such as Baal and Asherah, the first of the Ten Commandments specifically calls the Israelites to worship and serve Yahweh alone.*
>
> *Today, a general belief in the transcendent, with a move away from any commitment to doctrine and dogma, is replacing the traditional Christian worldview. Oddly, the pursuit for truth is coupled with a readiness to believe in almost any alternative occult teaching, especially if it is experiential.*

'If I may be so bold as to say so, my gods were merely superstitions. It may be fashionable for you and your postmodern, multi-culturalist outlook to affirm all cultures and religions, but has it occurred to you that in the very affirming of them you destroy them all? To say that everything is acceptable is not consistent. You see, there is no common frame of reference within a diversity of religions or cultures. To accept everything ultimately means that nothing is unacceptable. I know, because I've been there. It is a dangerous position to hold, and rather than bringing liberation, it brings enslavement. If there are no absolutes, there is no moral criteria beyond choice ...'

CyberCindy interrupts Ruth's sermon angrily, 'Who cares whether I am consistent or not? There is no guarantee that logic liberates!'

> The emancipatory role of reason was central to modernity, but the events of the twentieth century have made appeal to reason implausible.[50]

CyberCindy continues, 'I am free to be whatever I want to be now I can be certain there is no certainty! I am incredulous that you think your Yahweh God has all the answers! Ruth, you can't tell me you had any real choice. Your decision to turn to Naomi's god was merely a product of the structures and expectations around you.'

'That's just where you are wrong, CyberCindy! My commitment to Yahweh wasn't just from one religion to another. It was from a position of ignorance to one of wisdom, because I gave myself to the Creator of the world and of all things within it.'

Freedom

Personal liberty is doing as I please
Political liberty is voting for whom I please
Physical liberty is eating what I please,
Exercising when I please (or not at all),
Making love to whom I please,
Going where I please.
Intellectual liberty is thinking as I please,
Reading what I please,
Hearing what I please,
Seeing what I please,
Saying what I please,
Emotional liberty is feeling how I please,
Reacting how I please.
Spiritual liberty is Freedom![51]

> This is the message we have heard from him and declare to you: God is light: in him there is no darkness at all (1 John 1:5)

'Yahweh cares for all his creation, and he cares for justice, which means he is on the side of the oppressed. (Another irony.) My story is how the Almighty God cares for the smallest features of our lives, and also for those with the least status.'

'Well, I'm sorry Ruth but I don't see it that way. If God cares so much for justice and the oppressed, then why is there so much evil in the world?'

> Berkouwer identifies three factors that pose a challenge to a faith in the providence of God: other gods, a split culture and the problem of evil.[52]

blue

,

The Reason

My life is vile
I hate it so
I'll wait awhile
And then I'll go.
Why wait at all?
Hope springs alive,
Good may befall
I yet may thrive.
It is because I can't make up my mind
If God is good, impotent or unkind.[53]

'The problem of evil stems mostly from our lack of relationship with God – we generally choose to ignore God. People choose to do whatever they like, without reference to the living God. When people are alienated from God; they are alienated from one another. And the result is oppression, polarisation, isolation and disruption. I had choice. You have choice; we all have choice. Orpah returned home, to her gods.'

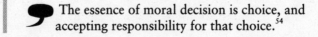 The essence of moral decision is choice, and accepting responsibility for that choice.[54]

As CyberCindy listens, a barrier of irritation and silent anger forms in her heart; what began as a pursuit for truth is now transforming into a lecture, where she is the pupil. This CyberCindy perceives, is a violation of her personal right to freedom of opinion and thought. She thinks Ruth smug and secure, that she can't really answer the problem of evil at all, but only talk around it, blaming everybody for it apart from herself. How dare Ruth imply that lack of relationship with God means lack of relationship with people? CyberCindy thinks of the many friends in her life, and rejects Ruth's analysis. CyberCindy is in no way oppressed, isolated or alienated. Ruth, so it appears to CyberCindy, is seeking to elevate herself at the expense of others. And yet Ruth's words are still affective: deep down, CyberCindy is disturbed, which is an unexpected and unwelcome intrusion into her psyche.

red

CyberCindy changes track. With a trace of venom in her voice she seeks to provoke Ruth, 'I have heard it said that "a woman will always sacrifice herself if given the opportunity – it's her favourite form of self-indulgence."[55] Why did you voluntarily choose to be Naomi's doormat?'

Ruth flushes with anger at the question. She remembers the painful time she had been through which had led to the realisation that the negation of self was women's sinfulness, along with the internalisation of blame and guilt. She had long ago recognised that women are thought to become godly by having no self of their own, and become 'suffering servants' by accepting male abuse and exploitation. This she had refused to give in to, preferring rather to affirm the 'grounded self' within her, relating to others in mutual service.[56]

Whilst feminist work on gender is diverse, it generally seeks to identify and challenge men's power over women, because feminists have political commitments to the empowerment of women.[57] But the Christian view of liberation is of freedom from sin before God. Sexual stereotyping is woven into society's fabric; but a real commitment of faith to the costly way which Christ outlined and fulfilled supersedes culture. Christ extends the boundaries of female and male stereotyping; true discipleship is costly because it demands action from both men and women to challenge assumptions and presuppositions, not in order to attain power, but rather in order to pursue 'shalom', and to become Christ-like.[58]

(Shalom: wholeness, order, well-being.)

'For a long time, CyberCindy, people have used my narrative to vindicate the notion that woman's nature equips them for serving others. I, Ruth, am upheld as a role model for women to follow, because I am prepared to put aside my own needs in order to serve others ... namely Naomi. But it is costly for male or female to deny themselves in the service of others. As Boaz implies, what I did was (possibly) exceptional (Ruth 2:11). But it had nothing to do with my gender. It was to do with my love for God, and for God's people, Israel. I gave myself to Yahweh, and in doing so I realized I do not need to strive after sexual fulfilment, male protection nor husband or children. I discovered my identity when I, Ruth the Moabite, through my loyalty to Naomi, and to her people, pledged myself to her God. I did not accompany Naomi in an effort to find a husband; I accompanied her because I was convinced that her destiny really was in the hands of her God. She also needed looking after in a world that was biased against childless widows. Naomi and I had much in common. We had nothing to lose, because we had already lost everything.'

CyberCindy was unimpressed, and continued her attack, 'Some say that the role of women is the "beautiful task of serving", whilst for men, their role is the "heavy task of ruling".[59] I think you have to take some of the blame for this. I don't see any deviation from that understanding in the book of Ruth. Boaz is proud; you are servile. Boaz is the upstanding local gentleman who makes decisions and gets things done. You are just a pawn in the story because of the system. How can you say that gender doesn't matter to you? Whatever you tell me about your identity in God, you ended up married, and a mother, and you used your body to achieve your own ends. It's just your word against some interpreter's that your primary motive was love for God. I think you were out to get hitched!'

CyberCindy is hopeful that an ideology that questions all ideologies will at last give her some significance in the world. The irony is that CyberCindy is willing to forsake her own gender in order to find self-value and self-esteem. She hankers after androgyny and criticises those who polarise the sexes. In so doing, she is unwittingly embracing patriarchal society by allowing her feminine sexuality to become blurred.

> ❜ Far from women's natural place being in the home, it has taken considerable efforts by men, the state, and a powerful patriarchal ideology to keep women out of public life.[60]

> ❜ 'It can be argued that the domination of women throughout most of human history has depended on the freeing of males for cultural control by filling women's days with most of the tasks of domestic production and reproduction.[61]

CyberCindy continued, 'If you wanted to prove to me that you had 'self-actualised' through your relationship with God, you would not have feared what the people of Bethlehem thought of you and your gods. Why couldn't you go there, accepting your differences, instead of conforming to their society?'

There was a pause before CyberCindy added, a little spitefully, 'I think you are a weak woman.'

Ruth sighed. CyberCindy had missed the point. Only the God of the Israelites could secure her identity, because it was he who was the creator god, the God of providence. Whilst CyberCindy was right to say that she should have stuck up for beliefs in a society which was alien to them, it was only through joining the Israelite community and committing herself to their God that Ruth had found her worth at all.

Besides which, Ruth was aware too that her decision had not been entirely rational; there had been an element in her conversion which was beyond her. Having committed herself to Yahweh, when she looked back at her life she could see that her conversion had been inevitable.

Ruth was beginning to realise that postmodernity had very little to say on the oppression of women in society; its primary dogma was to pursue and punish dogma. To further the cause of feminism was outside its remit. Ruth was becoming aware that for all its talk of deconstructionism, there is little evidence to show that postmodernity will change the role of women in society, because men dominate society.

> Dominant groups have no need to learn the non-dominant positions, because they can choose to remain unaffected by them.[62]

violet

Ruth turns to CyberCindy and says softly, 'Rebirth is only possible when we meet terror face-to-face.'[63]

CyberCindy is content to criticise Ruth and Boaz for their apparent gender roles in the story; she still has not accepted that Ruth, in her commitment to God and to Naomi, has radically overturned convention, something which is very dear to her own heart.

CyberCindy's attack on Ruth has not succeeded. She finds herself threatened because Ruth seems to have grasped something that CyberCindy cannot grasp. CyberCindy therefore decides to escape from this oppressive environment. She flicks a switch on her belt and raises her arm to enable her to fly back to the entry gate, leaving Ruth staring after her. But as she skims towards the gate, she suddenly remembers something, and taps in 3:13 on the gate console, quietly laughing to herself. CyberCindy is going to have some fun. She rejoins Ruth, but this time meets her on the threshing floor.

A Recap of Ruth 3 for the Reader

Ruth had, on Naomi's instruction, made herself beautiful and put on her best clothes, and gone to the threshing floor at night and in secret, to lie at Boaz's feet and await his instruction. Boaz wakes up in the night, startled to find a woman lying at his feet. She introduces herself and asks Boaz to, 'spread the corner of your garment over me'. Boaz commends her for her kindness in requesting this, observing that she has not gone after other men whether young or old, and also says what a good reputation Ruth has in the town, as a noble woman. But he tells Ruth there is another kinsman-redeemer, closer to Naomi and herself, than he. Boaz pledges to ask this fellow if he will redeem, and if so then Boaz is content to let the other kinsman-redeemer redeem. Ruth stays the night with Boaz, and early in the morning he sends her on her way with a shawl full of barley – another reminder that the women are still hungry and destitute. On her return home, Ruth tells Naomi what happened, and the chapter closes with Naomi confident that Boaz will settle the matter that day.

> **?** *As the Hebrew word for feet – regel – is sometimes used as a euphemism for the sexual organs in the Old Testament, there is some ambiguity for modern readers as to what really happened. Was there a sexual encounter? There is an inevitable distance, of culture, values and assumptions between ourselves and the storyteller from a different age, a different point in time. It is difficult to identify conclusively what common assumptions the storyteller shared with the original audience. In the story of Ruth we want to know what really happened, but we are not given a full account. Also, our understanding of the laws regarding levirate marriage, the role of the go'el and land rites is restricted by our limited knowledge.*
>
> *If an Old Testament man had intercourse with a woman he was obliged to marry her. The threshing floor scene is ambiguous because of what it doesn't say, rather than what it does say. There is no mention*

of Naomi's land in Ruth 3, even though in the next chapter Boaz's main concern is apparently the redemption of it. All we are told in the narrative is that Ruth appeals to Boaz to spread the corner of his garment over her. Most commentators are agreed that this constitutes an appeal for Boaz's protection by way of asking him to marry her – which is why he responds by acclaiming her kindness. She was not bound to seek a levirate marriage. (See notes on pages 60ff. and 69ff.). But she is faithful to Naomi and to her husband, and is anxious to further the family line in order to bring about Naomi's restitution, and the material security of both women. Had Naomi still been of childbearing age, then it would have been her role to seek Boaz out as her levir. Ruth's commitment to Naomi and to God's people is thus shown to be absolute, and Yahweh accomplishes his eternal purposes through her as a consequence.

'Psst!'

Ruth stirs from her sleep and looks around.

'CyberCindy!'

'What are you doing here, Ruth?'

'I'm trying to get some sleep. What are you doing here, is more the point. I thought you had given up on me.'

'Yeah, well, I think I might, but not just yet. The thing is, Ruth, postmodernity is post-feminist; feminism isn't my bag.' A pause, then, 'C'mon, Ruth, what are you doing here? Everybody who reads you wants to know!'

'Isn't it plain to see? I'm securing my future, Naomi's future, Boaz's future and all Israel's future.'

CyberCindy responds, 'Boaz seems to have a fine future to me. He's a wealthy man of social standing in a patriarchal society; and now he has you in his bed. How are you helping him secure his future?'

'I'm enabling him to fulfil his obligations and I'm helping him to play his part in redemption.'

'Obligations? Redemption?'

> **?** *CyberCindy doesn't understand the words because whilst individualism emancipates from social order it confines us to 'the solitude of our own hearts'.*[64] *'It removes the heroic dimension of life, the purpose worth dying for.'*[65]

'Please don't be naive, CyberCindy. Naomi and I have been in Bethlehem for about three months now, and no one has come to our aid, apart from Boaz. With the end of the harvest season, Naomi and I could look forward to destitution, for I would have had no work. If I hadn't chanced to work in Boaz's field, then I doubt if even he would have helped us. In fact I think he was only kind to me because he felt guilty.'

'Guilty?'

> **?** *'Guilty' is another word that is alien to CyberCindy's psyche. If there are no absolutes and no ideals, there is no guilt.*

'Yes. Boaz likes to have the respect of the community. But he hasn't acted to redeem Naomi because he is not the closest kinsman redeemer, and the closest kinsman redeemer probably hasn't acted to redeem Naomi because he has a legal right to Elimelech's property in any case. Boaz's challenge to him is to redeem, to buy back, the land in Elimelech's name and thus save us from destitution. But when the nearest kinsman redeemer realises that I am part of the deal too and that if I have a son the land will return to Elimelech's line, he sees he is in a no win situation. Marriage with me hadn't occurred to Boaz – I am legally free to marry whoever will have me. When Boaz blessed me, I wondered if it was a bit of a show, you know, to make other people think what a lovely fellow he was. So when I asked him to spread the corner of his garment over me, it was to find out how much he was willing to be prepared to be the answer of his own prayers. It would have been nice if I hadn't had to do it, if Boaz had taken responsibility for us on his own initiative.'

> To be accused of the unjustified exercise of power over others is a direct and personal challenge, which requires a direct and personal change in behaviour. It is painful for men to have to take this message from women. The dominance of men is so pervasive that it does not need to be pointed out.[66]

But that is why it is me, and not him, who is the ultimate redeemer. What power does Naomi have to challenge this patriarchal society? As a widow and a woman, she can't negotiate at the city gate, neither can I. Besides which, Naomi has interpreted her circumstances as being the result of God's punishment and it is probable that everyone else has too. To care for her will be costly, with no recompense. So I offered myself to Boaz in Naomi's place, both as a surrogate for her and in my own right, as the widow of Mahlon.'

? *Rabbis had difficulty justifying Boaz's marriage to Ruth, because of the stipulation in Deuteronomy 23:3–6, but did so by arguing that it referred to males only. This once again reinforces the (generally subconscious) argument that only men play a leading role in redemption.*

No Ammonite or Moabite or any of his descendants may enter the assembly of the Lord, even down to the tenth generation. For they did not come to meet you with bread and water on your way when you came out of Egypt, and they hired Balaam son of Beor from Pethor in Aram Naharaim to pronounce a curse on you. However, the Lord your God would not listen to Balaam but turned the curse into a blessing for you, because the Lord your God loves you. Do not seek a treaty of friendship with them as long as you live (Deuteronomy 23:3–6).

? *It is beyond doubt that Naomi owes her restoration to Ruth the Moabite woman. But Boaz too, has played an essential part, and the image of the three characters, interdependent on one another as their future is carved out gives us some insight into what can be achieved through love, fidelity and obedience, when people are committed to living in community.*

❟ Whilst Christianity has never denied equality of men and women in Christ, it has interpreted it in a spiritual and eschatological way, suppressing its relevance for the sociology of the church.[67]

(Eschatological: looking towards end times: death, judgement,
heaven and hell.)

'So, let me get this straight. You think you're the key
player in this story, but really you would rather it if Boaz
had recognised that you were a poor little foreign female
and taken pity on you without you having to go to him?'

indigo

Ruth paused, taken aback at this interpretation.

'What else was I to do? CyberCindy, women are the responsibility of men in Israelite culture. When women are allowed to become hungry it is because men are not fulfilling their duties. I do not have the luxury of independence which twenty-first-century women have. Boaz is a good man, he helped Naomi and I, but with the barley harvest over, our future was bleak.'

'But I thought Boaz loved you!'

'Love?', Ruth laughs, 'Boaz is perfectly happy for the closer kinsman redeemer to redeem! He knew that Elimelech's family had a duty towards Naomi, and felt bad that no one was doing anything. But it wasn't his immediate responsibility, and he didn't want Naomi anyway. Besides, Boaz was good to us – it's just that he wasn't as good as he could have been. Once he realised he could solve the problem by marrying me, and getting the land as well, he was quite happy.'

'So much for joining God's people then, if that's the way they treat you.'

'Sometimes God's people need a little stirring up. That's OK. That's why I'm in Scripture. You see, I know that Yahweh is on the side of justice, so I can trust him.'

Just then Boaz stirred in his sleep. Ruth and CyberCindy turned to look at him. He grunted and then, having got comfortable, began to breath deeply once more.

'Have I persuaded you at all, CyberCindy?', Ruth asks, earnestly.

'I don't know,' CyberCindy answers, her frustration echoing through each word, 'My situation isn't the same as yours. What you say may not be what I hear or even what I want to hear.'

> **?** *It is hard to know another person if truth is relative; it is perhaps even harder to know oneself. Communication becomes difficult. What was said and meant is re-interpreted to become what an individual may choose to receive. In a fragmented world, where there are few common understandings, arbitrary meaning inevitably leads to a breakdown in relationships.*
>
> *In her teens, CyberCindy had been hoping to discover her true, higher self and to transcend the social context in which she lived, but she has since concluded that there is no inner self to find and that there is no essence from which to be alienated.*
>
> *Parallelism, rather than alienation, is one of the characteristics of postmodernity. Ruth's commitment to justice and responsibility for others is a new phenomenon to CyberCindy, who is inclined to 'fight for the right to be herself', and yet she is still trying to discover who that self is.*

CyberCindy, gathering together her random thoughts, concludes, 'You are a foreigner who has severed your family ties. I too have lost my roots, my sense of community. The fragmentation of society that began at the end of the twentieth century has destabilised my environment. Your environment is unstable too. I try to find my identity by integrating my micro-cosmos, my little world, with the macro-cosmos, or by belonging to some group or fighting for a cause. Well, perhaps, when you joined the Israelites, that was what you were doing too. The difference is that your community is God-centred. You claim to be a redeemer; I have no need of redemption because my life is my own.'

> God the Holy Trinity is community and in that community of love we find our identity in the postmodern sea of shifting images and personal fragmentation.[68]

As she was speaking CyberCindy remembered what she had concluded in her adolescence: that totalitarian ideologies were damaging, and Western civilisation, with its absolutes and universal principles, had produced racism, imperialism, sexism, homophobia. The answer was, she had decided, to fight for the right to disunity, and to make sure that minority voices could be heard. She said as much to Ruth.

'Oh, CyberCindy! Don't withdraw into a ghetto! We all share a common humanity you know!'

'Oh yeah?', CyberCindy scoffs, 'What about the twelve tribes of Israel then? Aren't they a perfect example of ghetto and tribal warfare?'

> Without a moral framework, society disintegrates into warring factions, and isolated depraved individuals. The result is a replay of the violence, perversion, and anarchy described in the book of Judges, which at once diagnoses the moral collapse of ancient Palestine and precisely defines the postmodernist ethical theory (Judges 21:15).[69]

Ruth looks askance at CyberCindy, 'You've been reading other parts of the Bible!'

'What if I have?', CyberCindy retorts.

Ruth smiles knowingly.

'I may be only a small story, but I do play an important role in the whole big story of the Bible. I'm glad you've begun to look at the rest of Scripture.'

CyberCindy immediately feels vulnerable, and a little bit sick in her gut at the thought that Ruth might be winning her argument. All this interactive dialogue is beginning to have its effect. But despite the awful foreboding in her stomach, she recognises – just for a second – that perhaps she does need to consider the possibility that life is a story, which really does have an author. The thought slips into her mind uninvited and she wonders for a moment how her own actions impact on God. But the intrusive thought slips away again as quickly as it came; CyberCindy is afraid of beginning to care, of finding value.

> If self-esteem and self worth are based on illusions and self-alienating values, the inevitable result is isolation within, and the loss and denial of depth is regarded as normal.
>
> The ability to feel deep emotion is spasmodic and brief, partly due to information overload and partly due to the fragmentation of consciousness.[70]

green

CyberCindy is exasperated. Her postmodern
philosophy, more subconscious than it was conscious,
was one of aesthetics over ethics, style over content. It
had not been her intention to let Ruth know that she
had dipped into the book of Judges, even if Ruth was
merely a conglomeration of microchips and
imagination.

Whilst appeal to notions of right and wrong were largely
based, she thought, on individual interpretation, she
found to her confusion that her heart and imagination
had been touched by something greater than a
metanarrative or a rational argument. She was being
churned-up internally, but she didn't know where the
source of her discontent lay. She acknowledged that she
both respected Ruth and found her grossly irritating. But
in finding herself in relationship with this character of the
Bible, she had come alive to the possibility (and as yet it
was only a possibility) that God's providence was
potentially an immanent and painful fact of life. Having
unintentionally succumbed to this possibility,
CyberCindy takes control of her thought world and
reminds herself that whereas in the past she had thought
of God as some kindly force or power, now she is not
convinced that there is any God at all.

'For pity's sake,' she thinks to herself, 'Ruth is only a
fictitious character, an invention of some pathetic web
engineer. She isn't real. She's just a figment of someone's
imagination. Why do I let her influence me so much?'

Ruth's words echo in her ears, 'I may be only a small story, but I do play an important role in the whole big story of the Bible. I'm glad you've begun to look at the rest of Scripture.'

CyberCindy looks at Ruth. Ruth looks back at her, her lips curling attractively, in an all-knowing smile.

'You're just a figment of someone's imagination!', CyberCindy blurts out. Ruth's face turns pale. After a moment she appeals to CyberCindy with her deep, honest eyes, 'Is that what you really think? Is that what you really believe, CyberCindy?'

CyberCindy knows she is being irrational. She knows that she is speaking to a creation, to a character controlled by chips and electricity, a cyber robot. And yet she cannot tell Ruth to her face that she doesn't believe her. She is unwilling to respond. Rather than reply she chooses to exit Ruth, this time selecting to leave via parachute. This gives her the immediate exhilaration she desires, and she free falls rapidly away from Ruth's claustrophobic company. After tumbling uncontrollably for some seconds, the parachute suddenly, automatically, bursts open above her, so that CyberCindy floats down and away from the virtual world of Ruth in wilful rejection of all that she experienced.

The green light on the Safety-net Valve in CyberCindy's flat flickers frantically; the swift change from one world to another puts her computer system under considerable strain. CyberCindy, standing before her equipment, and blinded to her flat by the SceneSensa encasing her head, sways strangely to and fro, her body rhythmically motioning, rather like a giant praying mantis preparing to mate. Within the SceneSensa, CyberCindy witnesses a dramatic change from a hot barren climate to that of

95

mild blue skies and green trees, shade upon shade creating a great green sea below her. In between the trees untidy hedges frame large yellow fields and a cluster of red-roofed houses huddle to CyberCindy's right. A road, curling through the countryside, looks like a ribbon that somebody once dropped and CyberCindy notices a car weaving towards the houses, reminding her of some insignificant insect scurrying to its destiny.

yellow

CyberCindy is unwilling just now to confront what has been revealed to her; that is, to acknowledge that already her appetite for things spiritual has been both whetted by her encounter with Ruth and also thrust into turmoil by it. She does not know what to do with the surge of real feeling flowing in her blood. Before now, CyberCindy had been content with the inevitable meaninglessness of life. She had been content to concern herself with her work that she found flexible and challenging, and gave her a good income. With that income she could more or less choose to do whatever she liked, having no responsibilities and no dependants. She had friends; she met them now and then; they were no hassle to her and she was no hassle to them. She had no desire to be earnest about anything. She was carefree. Best of all, she had been happy. Hadn't she? She had been happy buying clothes she liked, the make-up she liked. She had been happy choosing and creating an image for herself to project to the world. She had been happy discovering new experiences. But now her foray into virtual reality was becoming virtually real and CyberCindy was neither prepared nor happy about the unexpected change that was taking place in her thinking as she met Ruth.

The parachute jump is over quickly and CyberCindy prepares to land, the grass below her getting nearer at great speed. She meets the earth with a thud, her knees caving in at the sudden jolt. She bangs her knee on the desk in front of her, which not only hurts but also sends tiny electric waves across her thigh. She lets out a scream of pain, and once she gets the all clear from the Heartthrob, tugs at her Grips and her SceneSensa impatiently before unzipping her Rompacomp to examine her leg. She is sure she will have a bruise on her knee; and her leg is covered in an unattractive blotch where the fibre-optic nerves on her Rompacomp hit her skin with harsh velocity. Her leg is stinging. Her mind is racing. CyberCindy feels helpless and isolated; she feels wounded and consumed with self-pity.

'Is that what you really think? Is that what you really believe, CyberCindy?', she remembers Ruth's face, the eyes seeking her out, the unspoken but evident disbelief in Ruth's voice as she asked the questions.

CyberCindy doesn't know what she thinks anymore, and she doesn't know what she believes. She is cross with herself that she ever began this caper. She thrusts herself on to her bed, her face hitting the soft, cool pillow with force in a mixture of anger, frustration and confusion. Her mind is a whirl of images and words. Her heart is fearful. Her leg hurts. After lying on the bed for some time – she does not know how long – CyberCindy begins to cry. She doesn't know why she cries, she just cries. All she is conscious of is a huge sadness overwhelming her, a lonely, aching sadness that is mourning for the CyberCindy she was before she ventured into Ruth. She wants to be that person still, but she cannot. Something has changed.

After there are no more tears left to cry, CyberCindy becomes conscious that she is cold. She wraps her duvet around her and curls up in a foetal position. She tries to take control, think things through. As she lies, snuggled in bed, snapshots of her childhood pass through her mind. She recalls her Mum and Dad kissing by the Christmas tree, surrounded by shimmering baubles and glitzy tinsel. She can't quite focus on her father's face; it's a blur. She can see up her mother's legs. Confusion, exclusion, the carpet rough on her skin, presents under the tree. Her parents' heads nearly touch the ceiling. Later, snow outside, there's a cold bed, damp clothes. A chair – her chair – knocked over. Shouting, loud and uninhibited. Hatred screwed into her mothers face, no gentleness or laughter, just spite in eyes flashing with accusation. Her father shouting abusively, words cascading from his mouth in an avalanche of anger. Suddenly, awfully, his hands wrapped around her mother's neck, fingers squeezing tight, his face red with the effort, teeth large and menacing. CyberCindy rushes to her mother's defence – her father pushes her aside in one easy motion; she falls onto the settee, crushes her arm, lies afraid, confused. Then suddenly laughter, a tender touch on her mother's cheek.

She left them to it and crawled away.

She recalls her mother's friends – Simon, Dave and Paul. Sweets, large male laps. She remembers Alan. She had really liked him, had hoped he would be her dad. She trusted him, and he played games with her. She thought he would stay with them forever. But then he went away too, and CyberCindy learnt independence. People were good to be with, but they were transitory, unreliable, not forever. She sighs in the silence, and cuddles herself, yearning for a life that she had never had.

Oddly, as she lies on the bed, she catches the smell of her father's jacket, the same smell as when he embraced her goodbye, its fragrance stirring emotions within her that she had long since forgotten. She recalls lying on the grass watching the clouds after hearing that her father had died of AIDS. Wispy clouds which played games in the sky, and gently watched her grief from a distance, grief that she was unable to express through tears or words. Her father – dead – was just a memory. She couldn't even recall his face.

She lies on her back, gazing not at the sky but at the ceiling, observing the cracks spanning across it which have always reminded her of veins in an old hand, and slowly realises that there is a world out there which some force beyond herself, which she half consciously acknowledges is probably God, is asking her to love.

She is not sure if she can do it.

PART
TWO

orange

Not long after this, CyberCindy drives to her favourite shopping mall, and spends the day trying on clothes and looking at make-up. She needs a change of image. She buys three new hair dyes – a soft brown, named Pulp, a light purple named Damage and a deep red, named Dangerous. She buys two new lipsticks, a pair of new shoes, a bright top and a long steel-grey dress, which flows over her form and highlights no part of her. Once home she sends an e-mail to a friend she hasn't seen for a while. That night, the friend calls round. They experiment with make-up together; they eat popcorn, watch a video and then make love. It is pleasant enough while it lasts. The friend stays the night but in the morning leaves rather abruptly, having drunk the remaining orange juice in the fridge.

> Whilst modernity has been preoccupied with discipline and leisure, postmodernity is concerned with excess and pleasure.[71]

After a breakfast of cold pizza and a Mars Bar, eaten in the kitchen with the television on, CyberCindy boots up her computer and decides to surf the Internet, minus Rompacomp and accessories. Cyber travel is a pastime that CyberCindy is finding increasingly addictive. In an uncharacteristic desire to curb this invasive instinct, and because she cannot be bothered to put on all the gear just now, she decides to visit the Internet Relay Chat (IRC), a

103

cheap alternative to long distance telephone calls, and find someone – any one – to talk to. Before she begins surfing she checks her e-mails, which simultaneously appear on the screen in word form, whilst a voice speaks them out. She has one message. It reads:

GAL!
m)Ooo.. :-) is not enuff, :-X but I'm :-L—
Yours ever, Michaelxxxxx

And speaks,

'GET A LIFE! Thinking happy thoughts is not enough! I'll say nothing, but I'm drooling. Yours ever, Michael, kiss, kiss, kiss, kiss, kiss'

'Thanks, Toby' she mutters, smiling to herself. Michael is a friend she met a few years ago on the World Wide Web, and they converse periodically at spasmodic intervals. He lives in Australia. He has a penchant for emoticons, and short banal messages.

(Emoticons: emotional icons.)

'Reply?', Toby enquires.

'No, not just now,' CyberCindy answers. She is pleased Michael has contacted her, but does not want to reply to him just now. She is not sure what to say. And then rather than going to the IRC, she impulsively decides to dip into the New Testament on the Net to see what she can find there. She exits out of her e-mail message, and zooms into the World Wide Web, sure of the path she will take today, choosing Paranormal and scanning down the menu for Christianity.

Last night, whilst in bed with her lover, Ruth's words came back to CyberCindy and freewheeled around her mind.

... the birth of a baby boy who brings joy ... a *go'el* who redeems, ... Boaz ... spread ... his garment ... foretaste ... Holy Spirit ... overshadow ... Mary ... New Testament ... fuller interpretation ...

She says loudly, 'Bible,' then, 'New Testament,' and lightly taps the screen on the first book: the Gospel according to Matthew.

blue

A voice, thick and rich, with an African tang to it announces, 'A record of the genealogy of Jesus Christ the son of David, the son of Abraham.' As the words dance on to the page, orange fonts on a dark blue background, CyberCindy gets the impression that the words are going to be accompanied with music. But there is no music, and the voice continues.

Whacky! Ruth's story finishes with a genealogy and Matthew's Gospel begins with one. She makes a mental observation that these religious people seem hooked up on family history. Then CyberCindy listens to the passage, occasionally looking up to witness the graphics that are accompanying it. They are very simply, cut-out people that form a chart in the form of a family tree.

'Abraham was the father of Isaac, Isaac the father of Jacob, Jacob the father of Judah and his brothers. Judah the father of Perez and Zerah, whose mother was Tamar.'

Tamar and Perez – the names were vaguely familiar.

'Perez the father of Hezron, Hezron the father of Ram, Ram the father of Amminadab' (great name) 'Amminadab the father of Nahshon, Nahshon the father of Salmon, Salmon the father of Boaz, whose mother was Rahab, Boaz the father of Obed, whose mother was Ruth, Obed the father of Jesse, and Jesse the father of King David.'

'Boaz, whose mother was Rahab,' CyberCindy continues to look and listen,

'David was the father of Solomon, whose mother had
been Uriah's wife.'

CyberCindy wonders who Uriah was, and fleetingly
concludes that he must have been someone rather
important. But she has had enough of this, thinking that
a list of names is a very boring way to start a story. She
exits Matthew and determines to meet Ruth once again,
because she wants to get a handle on these biblical
genealogies. Succumbing to her addiction, her venture
into the Matthew's Gospel has motivated her to travel
into virtual reality once again.

As she puts on her virtual reality garb she vaguely wonders
what her electricity bill will be this quarter. She plugs into
the Safety-net Valve and gets the go ahead, the happy
musical tone triggering within her a delightful anticipation
of what is to come. She plugs her Rompacomp into the
Heartthrob and prepares herself for the journey.

Soon CyberCindy is travelling by virtual metro, the smell
of sweat, body odour and alcohol invading her nostrils
pervasively. The journey is different from the one she
took before; the man opposite her is obviously drunk; he
lurches from side to side, preoccupied with his own
thoughts, coughing like some erratic machine gun, and
making odd animal-like noises. Occasionally, he looks
over to where CyberCindy is sitting, eyeing her up, but
CyberCindy is confident that he will not disturb her. She
can tell from her user-sensor that she is the only one
travelling on this route. She looks out of the window to
see vast tall buildings flashing by, graffiti decorating the
walls and giving some relief from the dismal terrain. The
train joggles along at quite a speed.

CyberCindy has forgotten that last time she met Ruth in
virtual reality she came home feeling frustrated and

vulnerable. Today is a new day with new possibilities, new questions. As she arrives at the gate, she decides to encounter Ruth at 4:16, after the birth of Obed. She keys in the appropriate command and, fast-forwarding, enters the scene to find Naomi sitting in the shade of her home, a baby cradled in her arms making soft guttural noises, which delight Naomi out of all proportion. CyberCindy has never seen the sombre Naomi looking so buoyant and bubbly, and she pauses for a while to admire the old woman, her tough, lined face exuding joy. Ruth is sitting nearby, cloaked with her usual confidence, grinding flour.

'CyberCindy!', she greets warmly, apparently bearing no grudge against her, 'So you've come to see the baby! You must have maternal instincts after all!'

Immediately, CyberCindy is irritated, and Ruth realises, too late, that she has made a mistake.

'I'm sorry, CyberCindy. I suppose I just find it rather hard to accept androgyny as being a realistic ontological state.'

(Ontological: state of being.)

CyberCindy isn't ready for argument. She just wants to have a bit of a chat, idle away some time. Nevertheless, she finds herself taking the bait, 'That is because you cling to an inaccurate polarisation of the sexes and their roles ...'.

Ruth doesn't reply and there follows a pause whilst CyberCindy wonders whether to continue in conversation or take a detour home via a different virtual world. She has heard it rumoured that there is a fantastic experience to be had in Orgasmaland, a territory where individuals can float, unidentified, and engage in anonymous and highly erotic sex. Even if she doesn't do that, she could always return to her flat and contact Australian Michael. And she really ought to empty the bin.

As CyberCindy reflects on the alternatives, she is surprised to discover that she still finds interaction with Ruth strangely compelling, for she decides to stay without very much heart searching. Despite their differences, Ruth's perspective on life seems to her to be more interesting and worthy of time investment than anything else. Ignoring the debate which Ruth has just begun, she says, 'Ruth, I tried to read Matthew's Gospel this morning.'

Ruth grins, revealing that relaxed enthusiasm which so appeals to CyberCindy and so irritates her.

'But it's so boring, I only got as far as verse six. Why does it start with a genealogy? What's the big idea?'

Ruth is thoughtful before she expounds, 'Matthew begins his Gospel with a genealogy because historical roots are very important for Jews. And Matthew wanted his readers to see that everything that has happened in Jewish history finds its fulfilment in Jesus. My story is one of God's providence, and so is Matthew's. He wants his audience to know, right from the beginning, that God's purposes have been fulfilled through Jesus.'

'But Ruth, how does a list of names prove God's purposes?'

'Jewish children are brought up on Jewish history. These names, and the stories behind them, would be familiar to Matthew's hearers.' Ruth pauses again, whilst she pounds the grain in the bowl, 'Did you see me in there?', she continues, coyly.

CyberCindy nods, 'Yeah, but what have you got to do with Jesus?'

Ruth doesn't like CyberCindy's attitude, but she is trying to love her in spite of it. 'I'm King David's great grandmother,' she says, as if it explains everything.

'Well, I could work that out from your genealogy, if that was what I wanted to know.'

'But Matthew's genealogy is different from my one.'

'Yes, it's longer,' CyberCindy volunteered, sniggering at her own joke.

Ruth continues, 'Matthew's genealogy shows that Jesus belongs to the legitimate line of the king of Israel. It shows that his roots go deep into Israel's sacred history, which God has been guiding, to its culmination. All Old Testament history leads towards the birth of the Messiah. You can see God's providence being worked out through the course of time. And what really interests me, CyberCindy, is that Matthew mentions women – and I am one of them – and they all have rather dubious biographies.'

(Biblical genealogies are almost always given in the father's line.)

'Tamar's story can be found in Genesis 38, Rahab's story in Joshua 2, and Uriah's wife, Solomon's mother, was Bathsheba, who committed adultery with King David. You can find their story in 2 Samuel 11. And why are they cited, together with me, great grandmother to King David, and ancestor to the Messiah? Some people say it is because there is a shocking nature behind our stories which foreshadows the redemption which will be offered to sinners like us....it does seem a little odd to me that he doesn't mention Sarah, Abraham's wife.'

'Sinners?', CyberCindy interrupts.

Ruth ignores her, for she doesn't want to get sidetracked at this point.

'But some of the men had just as dubious backgrounds, if not more so. Manasseh was reckoned to be one of the most evil kings of all time. And David effectively had Uriah murdered, for the love of lust. I don't think women can be singled out as being particularly sinful.'

'Sinful?', CyberCindy asks, again.

Ruth meets CyberCindy's eyes. She doesn't want to put her off with the mention of sin, and she doesn't want to avoid it. But she knows that CyberCindy cannot come to terms with the notion of sin.

'But, of course, Mary is a young virgin, with no chequered history behind her. And she is an Israelite, not like Rahab or me. Bathsheba was probably a gentile, because her husband was a Hittite and Tamar was probably a gentile too. I think Matthew was probably making the point that the gospel was going to be for all peoples, whatever their background, not remain exclusive for the Jews.'

'Well, why couldn't he just say that at the start of his book, in plain English?'

'Matthew wanted to show, through Jewish history, that these four women in the genealogy are vehicles of God's messianic plan in spite of their irregular circumstances … and so is Mary.'

CyberCindy is becoming increasingly frustrated. She is concious of a soft ringing in her ears and wonders if she has set the volume too loud; but to adjust it would mean coming out of Ruth and into the mundane. She realises that Ruth sees things from an entirely different perspective to her own – how she can categorise someone's life as being one of 'irregular circumstances' is

111

something she just can't connect with. But she lets the statement go, and instead follows up on Mary.

'Mary?'

'The mother of Jesus. All the women had ambiguous, or irregular, sexual relationships with the men involved. But there was something extraordinary going on while God worked out his purposes nonetheless. Mary's pregnancy could have caused a scandal, for she became pregnant outside of marriage. Suspicions of illegitimacy would have slurred the name of Jesus.'

'Why?'

> ? *CyberCindy's question is a genuine one, for she sees no scandal in illegitimacy. For her, marriage is for those who choose it. A lifelong, permanent relationship holds no attraction to CyberCindy, who views marriage as a constraining institution which society perpetuates for its own purposes – in order to legitimise oppression, enforce law and order, and to control. In any case, in her experience, relationships are not capable of being sustained. Whilst she has many friends, she doesn't expect to maintain them throughout her life. The future is uncertain.*

Ruth doesn't know how to answer CyberCindy's simple question; she is at a loss for words. She has presumed shared moral values, and has argued from her own position.

> ? *It is hard to argue about moral issues when no common ideological framework can be assumed. Postmodernity emphasises difference, differentiation and fragmentation, and diversity is understood to be good. Whilst differing opinions*

can be respected, any suggestion that humanity inherently shares agreed ethical values is considered naïve. There is no common core of morality. There are no shared ethical values. Fragmentation is the order of the day.

'Well, CyberCindy,' she says after a little reflection, 'I suppose we have to accept that we are different. We live in different times and cultures and our whole horizons are governed by a set of different assumptions and sociological circumstances.'

> The little paths we trace between dawn and dusk are quite different if timetables, clocks and computers, rather than seasons, sunrise and nightfall, frame our coming and going.[72]

'Earlier on, you tried to argue that the age you live in was much the same as mine,' CyberCindy mused, mischievously.

'Well, I still do think there are great similarities. But for the moment, will you just be content to understand that Matthew, in his genealogy, was trying to express the greatness of God's grace, that it was for all and would extend from Jew to Gentile, to men and women of high or low status, and that the birth of Jesus Christ has universal significance?'

'No!', CyberCindy replied quickly, 'No, I won't! What about Buddhism and Hinduism?'

> From the standpoint of Jesus Christ, the non-Christian religions seem like stammering words from some half-forgotten saying: none of them is without a breath of the Holy, and yet none

> of them is the Holy. None of them is without its
> impressive truth, and yet none of them is the truth:
> for their truth is Jesus Christ.[73]

'I think it is more important to recognise that others can possess truth than it is to ram your own version of it down other people's throat!', she continues heatedly. (It is unusual for CyberCindy to feel passion. She is finding herself to be surprisingly intolerant. Why does Ruth produce this reaction in her?)

'I haven't tried to ram it down your throat,' Ruth retaliated sharply, 'you asked me.'

'All you offer is glib, know-it-all answers.'

'Glib answers?', Ruth is incredulous now, for the case she has presented to CyberCindy is one which she had perceived as being full of integrity and genuine reason.

'Yes, glib! Like saying that Jesus has universal significance. I don't see his significance at all! Jesus has no significance to people in the real world! You, Ruth, you're just living in a vacuum, in an imaginary world where reality doesn't exist! I don't care if he was illegitimate or not, and neither does the rest of the world! I don't see what your morals have to do with God!'

In her upset Ruth retorts uncharacteristically, 'Jesus has significance because he is God!'

indigo

The words punch the air with unexpected violence, and a silence, heavy and ominous, falls upon the women, disbelief bringing their encounter to a palpable crescendo. CyberCindy is staggered by the claim. Ruth is surprised too, but with herself. She never thought she would have the courage to vocalise her belief. It is easy sharing her faith with Naomi, a fellow believer, but CyberCindy she finds threatening.

CyberCindy quickly breaks the silence with a forced laugh. She is embarrassed for Ruth. She has to ask her,

'Ruth, how can you say that? How can you say that Jesus is God? You are incredible!!'

red

'I'm not incredible at all! It's what the Bible reveals! The church exists because Jesus is God! I exist because Jesus is God! You exist because Jesus is God!'

CyberCindy is confused and taken aback. She had not expected this outburst from Ruth and does not know how to react to her.

'Ruth, you're out of your mind,' CyberCindy comments, with a touch of sadness in her voice.

'And you're not?', Ruth asks, in rapid self-defence.

Both women feel sensitive and defensive. CyberCindy, genuinely curious, is not sure how to progress the conversation. Ruth, evidently humiliated, is not sure either. She grinds the flour with aggression and fights back tears. She so much wants CyberCindy to understand, she so much wants CyberCindy to grasp the treasure that she has grasped. She is not interested in winning a point in an argument here or there. For Ruth, her faith invades everything; she refuses to offer CyberCindy a designer religion with supplementary free gifts of nebulous spiritual insight that have no impact or relevance to practical ethics, politics, and economics. Ruth has a deep understanding of justice and truth, but she is also finding that life with God is abundant life; it makes her feel truly human. It hurts her that she cannot express herself properly to CyberCindy, who finds flaw in any argument she seeks to proffer.

116

CyberCindy notes internally that she does not want to escape from Ruth just now. In the past, she may have simply exited. But now she wants to hear her out. She waits, knowing that Ruth will seek to justify herself sooner or later. Her patience is soon rewarded. Ruth looks up imploringly, and says, 'CyberCindy, my friend, if Jesus is who he claims to be, and if he historically came to earth and ministered to historical people, and if he historically went to the cross and then historically rose again, it matters to everyone, dead or alive.'

'It doesn't matter to me,' CyberCindy retorts simply, 'I couldn't give a fig.'

'Oh, well,' Ruth paused. She is not quite sure where to take the conversation.

Then she asks, 'CyberCindy, tell me, what do you regard as truth?'

'Truth?', CyberCindy repeated. She doesn't have to ponder. 'Truth is what we believe to be true. It's as simple as that. Your truths are different from my truths.'

? *CyberCindy cannot grasp an ideology which seeks to promote objective Truth, she can only accommodate various truths at various times in her life. For she knows that everyone's experience is different. She is open to spiritual insights, but rejects any claims which seek to dominate or oppress by asserting unique, transcendent truth. Every opinion is a valid one, and no preferential treatment should be given to one understanding above that of another. Subjectivity is the only rational reality.*

In the background, Obed is gurgling with his grandmother, who is gaily reciting nursery rhymes, one after the other, whilst jogging the baby on her knee. Three women pass by, on their way to fetch water from the well. CyberCindy is conscious of one of them saying, 'Ruth is better to Naomi than seven sons.'

CyberCindy hears the words but doesn't see the women speak, and she is surprised that she is even within earshot. Whether it is Naomi playing with Obed, or the tribute from the women, or the heat of the day, or a delayed reaction to Ruth's proclamation, CyberCindy feels tired. She looks at Ruth, Naomi, Obed, and decides to get out, this time for good. What is she doing here? What began as an adventure, which she could control, is becoming an intrusion into her personal psyche – she doesn't like it and won't have it.

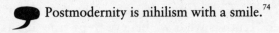 Postmodernity is nihilism with a smile.[74]

orange

On her way home, as she passes through Gibson transfer station and impulsively seeks out a free Bulletin Board. Once seated, she types, 'Who thinks Jesus is God? Sandy wants to know!', and then she waits.

? *CyberCindy uses a pseudonym when she plays with others on the Internet, for this gives her the freedom to create new and different identities for herself. When she wants conversation she often chooses the name Sandy, because it can be male or female. Whilst each pseudonym is in itself fictitious, she believes it reveals an aspect of her authentic personality. She has a multifaceted personality, which takes on different characteristics in different situations. Her life is compartmentalised, and each compartment is an entity in itself, in which she presents unique aspects of her own persona. CyberCindy does not constrain herself to any one particular identity, and in a given context she will draw on appropriate values, which in a different context she may dismiss. For example, at work CyberCindy knows that time equals money. She presents herself as an efficient, dynamic, individual, working to fine deadlines. Out of her working environment, CyberCindy adopts a very different approach. She is frequently late when meeting friends, because she has found something better to do beforehand; she eats when she is hungry and not*

*at predefined times in the day; she likes cybertravel
because it gives her an illusion of timelessness.
Sometimes, she likes to look polished and
sophisticated. She paints her nails on her fingers and
toes. At other times she likes to look outrageous and
wears sexually provocative clothes; at other times
again she will present as neat and naïve. Each image
she projects is designed to proclaim her current
philosophy on life; her desire; her mood.
CyberCindy is consistently inconsistent.*

A reply soon emanates from the screen, preceded by a
voluptuous androgynous face with shining black lips and
erotic eyes, shaded in stripes of blue, purple and black.
'Hi Sandy! Is Jesus God? Or: Is God Jesus? If God is
Jesus then we are all gods, for God was a human being.
From Mickey.'

She replies, 'Hi Mickey! God being Jesus is not the same
as Jesus being God. If Jesus is completely God then he
could never be completely human. Doesn't God have to
be more than human? From Sandy.'

As she waits for Mickey's reply, she receives a message
from a different punter, 'Sandy, who cares? Come with
me on the superhighway to Orgasmaland. Let's explore
God there. Susie.'

CyberCindy gazes at the Board, immobile. 'Come with
me on the superhighway to Orgasmaland. Let's explore
God there.' Her eyes read the words but they don't
connect. Her heart pumps in furious frustration.
Orgasmaland couldn't be further from where she wants
to be right now. She wants dialogue, not sexual
encounter. She wants people she can talk to; she wants
other opinions, other perspectives and other thoughts.

Fraught and frustrated, CyberCindy leaves the cyber-image winking at her on the screen, and slowly walks out of Gibson for the last part of her journey home. Once home she takes off her Rompacomp, thinking it has all become a bit too much of a rigmarole, and she sits down at her desk. She checks her e-mail. She is not going to get emotional about all this. It simply isn't worth it. She finds two messages waiting for her. One is from her employer, informing her that they will be moving addresses in two weeks time and will be entering a whole new phase of the project she has been engaged in, the other is a flame.

(Flame: a rude message.)

This is not what CyberCindy wants. She sits quietly before the screen, and stares at the message, as she did at the Bulletin Board at Gibson. She stares at it and wonders what life is all about. She has no energy to react to the message, no energy to care that somebody thinks it is funny to misuse and abuse the system. She leaves her desk and takes a shower, and then goes out for a walk. She hasn't done that for a very long time.

green

In the park, CyberCindy sees the sun shining through
the trees, the leaves glittering and twinkling as they
flutter in the wind. She feels the warm rays of the sun
on her skin. The wind, soft and gentle, is refreshing.
CyberCindy sits down on a wooden bench, noticing
the writing etched into the back support, 'In loving
memory of Ronald Spackman'. She finds herself
wondering who Ronald Spackman was, and who had
loving memories of him. She wondered if anyone
would ever have loving memories of her. She thought
of the friend who had stayed the night recently. She
knew their relationship was nothing very special, that
they were both using one another to pass away the
time; she knew that they didn't care for one another
particularly, not in any real sense. She thought of
Michael from Australia. Their relationship was only a
joint ego trip. She thought of her mother, with whom
she had lost contact a few years ago, and she thought
of her mother's live-in boyfriends, whom she had never
liked. She remembered her father. She only had a few
memories of him. One was feeling his skin as she rode
on his back in the water, in some lake, on holiday,
when she had been very young. Another was when he
lost his temper after she had spilt jelly on a new
carpet. How could anybody think Jesus was God? She
wonders how many people believe he is. Looking up
CyberCindy sees a man, shabby and hooded in a dirty
old anorak, too big for his frail frame, shuffling

determinedly towards her, his gnarled toes curled together in his sockless sandals. (Perhaps he is Jesus.)

'Fiver for a cuppa tea?', he asks. CyberCindy ignores him and hopes he will go away.

'Fiver for a cuppa tea?', he repeats. She looks at him and shakes her head negatively. He shuffles past, on to his next victim. CyberCindy watches him, detachedly. She wonders, fleetingly, what his life must be like. The thought interests her, but does not persist, for she does not possess the imagination, or even the knowledge, to participate in the squalor, the hunger and the destitution of the man.

CyberCindy blames society for producing tramps like him. There is nothing she can do to help. He is not her problem.

She leaves the bench and on the way home buys a Chicken Tikka from the takeaway. Back at her flat, CyberCindy finds she has lost her appetite, and throws most of the food, together with its elaborate packaging, into the bin. She sips at her glass of wine whilst gazing at the news and the programmes that follow, but her mind is not really engaged. She sleeps badly that night, and the next morning wakes up to discover that she has missed an important meeting for work in cyberspace, which she had made weeks ago.

'Is Jesus God?', the thought shadows her other thoughts, sometimes fading, sometimes clear and defined, 'What if he is? What if he isn't? Does it matter?'

? *It was about this time that the Engineer completed her work on John 4, and the virtual world of Sychar, featuring the Samaritan Woman at the Well went live, to much acclaim.*

Reader, choose to either:

F1 read Appendix 1 for essential background
      information to the text, from a modern perspective.[75]
F2 read on.
F3 pray.

> *Yet to all who received him, to those who believed in*
> *his name, he gave the right to become children of*
> *God – children born not of natural descent, nor of*
> *human decision or a husband's will, but born of God*
> *(John 1:12).*

yellow

,

I thirst for truth,
But shall not drink it till I reach the source.[76]

'Ruth, won't you come with me to meet Jesus?'
CyberCindy asks encouragingly, 'Wouldn't you just love
to meet him?'

She has recently invested in a new modem that enables the
cybernaut to superimpose one virtual world upon another,
and CyberCindy has a notion that she could facilitate a
conversation between the virtual Ruth and the virtual
Jesus. She is so excited by the prospect that she has
forgotten her resolve not to mess with Ruth anymore. The
thought intrigues and appeals and she can't wait to
experiment in cyberspace. She wants to witness Jesus'
reactions to Ruth's analysis of herself and also to see
Ruth's reaction to Jesus. Besides which, she is curious to
know how Jesus will be portrayed – will he be good
looking – fit, even – or will he be nondescript and mousy?

In answer to CyberCindy's invitation, Ruth answers quite
determinedly, 'If it is possible for me to meet Jesus,
CyberCindy, then I would like to do so.'

CyberCindy grins uncharacteristically, in triumph. They
are really going to go places now.

After a couple of abortive attempts to hook the virtual
world of Ruth on to her belt, CyberCindy succeeds in

125

exiting Ruth without leaving the panorama of ancient Israel behind her. CyberCindy calls up a routemaster gopher, and she and Ruth then travel to Westbound Port. CyberCindy and Ruth walk slowly but determinedly through other worlds, the familiar territory of heat, dust, white houses and blue sky creating a backdrop over which changing scenes pass. Soft colours make way for brighter ones, small shapes become gradually bigger, then round, then angular, the images passing one over the other, rather like a moving net curtain cascading fluently over a fixed scene. They pass through urban scenes, cartoon worlds, moonscapes, seascapes, motorways and weather reports. CyberCindy has turned the volume down, for she finds the combination of changing visual scenes accompanied by the appropriate noises that go with them rather disorientating.

As they travel, CyberCindy notices that Ruth is almost static, her legs being the only part of her that moves. She wonders fleetingly if they will crash, but the thought is dismissed as suddenly, with no warning, they arrive at a huge signpost, a gate, similar to the one CyberCindy encounters when she enters Ruth. On it, in huge green letters, is written, 'WELCOME TO SYCHAR' under which is the announcement, 'Enter Entirely at Your Own Risk. No responsibility can be taken for problems that are experiential in nature. Your statutory rights are not affected.' CyberCindy glances over towards Ruth, who slowly blinks and gradually begins to move, as if coming alive.

'Have we arrived?', Ruth asks.

'Arrived?', CyberCindy repeats, 'Oh, no. But we're getting there.' She smiles smugly.

? *To have arrived would mean the adventure was over. For CyberCindy this is only the beginning.*

CyberCindy unhooks Ruth from her belt, and is pleased to find she is still beside her on completion of the manoeuvre. Ruth's virtual world recedes into the background, fading gradually, until there is only one scene dominating CyberCindy's experience, but Ruth remains by her side as clear and sharp as ever. CyberCindy is thrilled with the moment, feeling herself to be something of an explorer.

On completion of entry, both women look about them.

The soil under their feet is hard and irregular, scattered with rocky stones, a worn carpet of grass struggling for survival through the unyielding earth. To their left are some sheep, their shaggy coats protecting them from the heat of the unrelenting sun. A sheep, larger than most, raises its head and stares at the two intruders. It bleats loudly, takes a couple of steps away from them, and then continues to pull at the grass, conscious of the visitors but unwilling to let them interrupt its feeding. Beyond the sheep a mountain stretches towards the sky in the distance, clusters of bushes, and rocky walls making abstract patterns on the dense earth. Closer to the women, small, irregular trees bunch together like enormous posies, and soften the terrain. To their right another mountain rises high on the horizon, small blocks of white portraying sites of habitation on the mountainside, exposing what appear to be little villages. The women are evidently in some sort of a valley, not far from a village themselves, for ahead of them, just around a bend in the road, but not far away, they see a small gathering of houses made from white stone. The heat permeates the scene; CyberCindy finds it stinging her nose and causing dryness about the mouth; she marvels at the clarity of colour and vision; it really is as if she were in another part of the world. She feels no longer like an explorer, but a tourist. Other people have been here before her, she is sure of that.

Past the sign, before the village, they see a well, and sitting beside the well is a man. As CyberCindy and Ruth watch, a woman approaches, a large water pot held on her head at an angle.

'Oh!', exclaims Ruth, 'Oh, CyberCindy, it's him!'

'Who?', asks CyberCindy, fearful at the new tremulousness in Ruth's voice.

'It's Jesus! He's going to talk to the Samaritan woman at the well!'

indigo

CyberCindy and Ruth eagerly approach the couple, Ruth's complexion turning a deeper than usual colour as the blood rushes to her face in anticipation and excitement. CyberCindy is slightly bemused, and privately determines to send an e-mail to the anonymous virtual world creators to commend them for the brilliant job they have done on this cyber creature. As they approach, however, there is no acknowledgement that they have been observed, and on getting nearer, CyberCindy hears the woman's resonant voice tumbling out of her active mouth in indignant tones.

'You are a Jew and I am a Samaritan woman. How can you ask me for a drink?'.[77] to which a voice replies calmly,

'If you knew the gift of God and who it is that asks you for a drink, you would have asked him and he would have given you living water.'[78]

CyberCindy's interest is aroused. The voice is mellow, rich, kind, generous, firm and authoritative. She wants to hear more.

Ruth suddenly lurches forward, away from CyberCindy and towards Jesus, 'Oh, yes sir, yes sir, give me living water!', but neither character before them responds, although both are still, as if the pause button has been pressed. CyberCindy watches.

'Jesus!', Ruth calls urgently, tentatively. There is no response. 'Jesus, my Lord!', Ruth calls again. The woman turns her head, looking straight towards Ruth, but no flicker of recognition graces her face, and she returns her eyes to Jesus.

'Sir', the woman says, 'You have nothing to draw with and the well is deep. Where can you get this living water? Are you greater than our father Jacob, who gave us the well and drank from it himself, as did also his sons and his flocks and herds?'[79]

Ruth calls out, 'Yes, he is greater! Of course he's greater! Listen to him, woman, listen to him and stop arguing will you?'

The woman glances towards Ruth once more, but again gives no reaction to the interruption. The face of Jesus remains obscured, and all that is visible is his Rabbi's cloak and his big, workmanlike hands, which, CyberCindy observes when they move, are unexpectedly dark and hairy.

'Everyone who drinks this water will be thirsty again, but whoever drinks the water I give him will never thirst. Indeed the water I give him will become in him a spring of water welling up to eternal life.'[80]

The woman pauses before she replies, 'Sir,' she says, 'give me this water so that I won't get thirsty and have to keep coming here to draw water.'[81]

'Wrong motive!', calls Ruth, 'You shouldn't want Jesus for what's in it for you! He's talking about eternal life, for goodness sake, not magic!'

Ruth is clearly frustrated, and CyberCindy finds herself in a strange situation. It would appear that they are able to witness the scene but not interact with it. That is clear enough. But what CyberCindy had not bargained for was Ruth's proactive engagement in the scene before them.

She had assumed it would be herself making the running, and is at a loss as to how it is that Ruth, a cyber world creation, can relate to these two new characters in a new world, without her stimulation. CyberCindy had imagined she would be a kind of 'go-between' between Ruth and Jesus. From some reason, which she cannot understand, this is not necessary. Perhaps the technology enabling interactive dialogue is more advanced than she thought. And yet they cannot make contact with the characters in the world of Sychar. It is all rather peculiar, but intriguing nonetheless. In any case, this unexpected reaction from Ruth adds to the thrill of the adventure; CyberCindy is not perturbed, merely mildly surprised.

'Ruth!', CyberCindy motions, 'I don't think they can hear you! There's something not right with the set up.'

Ruth glances back at CyberCindy, 'Oh, CyberCindy, I so much wanted to meet him, to see his face.'

Before CyberCindy has chance to respond, they hear Jesus say, 'Go, call your husband and come back.'[82]

violet

The woman answers, 'Sir, I have no husband.'[83]

'You are right in saying 'I have no husband', for you have had five husbands, and the one you have now is not your husband. What you have just said is true!'[84]

It is difficult for the observers to perceive the woman's reaction to Jesus' words. Her face is immobile and her eyes set themselves upon Jesus. After a pause, she speaks with an unforgiving determination.

'Sir, I see you are a prophet. Our ancestors worshipped on this mountain, but you say that the place where people must worship is in Jerusalem.'[85]

'Believe me, woman, a time is coming when you will worship the Father neither on this mountain nor in Jerusalem. You worship what you do not know; we worship what we know, for salvation is from the Jews. But the hour is coming and is now here, when the true worshippers will worship the Father in spirit and in truth, for the Father seeks such as these to worship him. God is spirit, and those who worship him must worship in spirit and truth.'[86]

The woman turns away, gazing at the mountain. In the background, a small group of men are approaching from the direction of the village, but she is oblivious to them, for her back is against them and her eyes are focussing on some imaginary future.

'I know that Messiah is coming, and when he comes, he will proclaim all things to us.'[87]

Jesus' voice, clear, firm and tender says simply 'I am he, the one who is speaking to you.'[88]

The woman looks at Jesus sharply, for she had been unprepared for the announcement. She wipes her perspiring brow with her sleeve, and Jesus echoing her action, does likewise. It really is very hot. The men approach the well, cautiously viewing Jesus and the woman. They seem a little awkward, even embarrassed.

The woman becomes conscious of their arrival, and turns quickly, hurrying off in the direction of the village, barely paying the men any attention at all. One of the men steps forward, and Jesus turns his head away from the woman, who he had watched as she left him, and to the man seeking his attention. 'Rabbi, eat something,'[89] says the man.

'I have food to eat that you know nothing about,'[90] Jesus says, cryptically.

CyberCindy wants to see Jesus' face, and is getting irritated that she is unable to view his expression, see his eyes, his nose, his lips. It is simply amateurish to produce a virtual world where it is not possible to engage with the primary character. She decides to complain to Highway Associates. Ruth's creators had paid attention to the finest details, right down to skin, tone and facial expression. It was pathetic that this virtual world had gone live before it was complete. Her adventure was costing her money; if they couldn't do better than this she would have to complain to the Virtual Reality Standards Council (the VRSC). If they got enough complaints they could sue the makers, and she may get some free cyber travel.

The disciples wander towards a tree, not far from the well, and sit down underneath it, sharing out the food they have just acquired from the village stores. They are clearly offended at Jesus' refusal to eat with them, and begin muttering amongst themselves, 'Surely, no one else has brought him something to eat? You don't think that Samaritan woman gave him food, do you?'

Jesus stays by the well initially, but after a few moments moves to join his friends, 'My food is to do the will of him who sent me and to complete his work. I know we have a saying "Four months more, and then the harvest", but I tell you, look around and see how the fields are ripe for harvesting. The reaper is already receiving wages and is gathering fruit for eternal life, so that sower and reaper may rejoice together. For here the saying holds true, "One sows and another reaps". I sent you to reap that for which you did not labour. Others have laboured and you have entered into their labour.'[91]

Just as Jesus finishes saying this, the woman returns, with a crowd of fellow villagers. She had evidently gone to seek them out and ask for their opinion of Jesus, the man who claimed to be the Messiah, who had proved this by his intimate knowledge of her life. An elderly man, evidently much respected by the crowd with him, stands forward and invites Jesus to stay with them for a while.

'My pleasure', CyberCindy hears Jesus reply. The men clustered under the tree look surprised and share glances of dismay, and possibly confusion, with one another.

Jesus and the crowd begin to walk in the direction of the houses, his back still being all that is on view.

orange

CyberCindy vents her frustration by kicking the earth. She stubs her toe, and lets out a yell of pain. She swears violently. Ruth observes the performance, a certain disdain on her face.

'We can't see Jesus, we can't talk to anyone, what's the point? What the hell do the makers think they're playing at? This is all a load of crap!'

Ruth turns away from the CyberCindy, offended by her language. She glances over to the well. The Samaritan woman, having introduced her people to Jesus, is standing towards the back of the crowd, her face radiant with excitement and joy.

'Excuse me!', Ruth calls, 'excuse me, could we talk with you?'

The woman turns towards Ruth and CyberCindy. CyberCindy is suddenly conscious of the bleating of the sheep, which seems extraordinarily loud, and the hubbub of excitement surrounding Jesus. For a moment, CyberCindy thinks the woman will ignore them as before, but contrary to these expectations, the woman turns around completely, and walks towards Ruth and CyberCindy, elegant, confident and serene. She is older than CyberCindy had first surmised; her face is round and plump with a gentle softness about her, wrinkles around her eyes and lips contrasting with the smoothness of her cheeks. Her mouth, large and domineering, curls downward at the edges, belying a certain arrogance, or edginess, but her eyes are sparkling with life. She looks Ruth up and down, 'You want to talk with me?'

'Yes,' Ruth answers simply, 'CyberCindy and I would love to meet you.'

The woman turns her gaze to CyberCindy. As they encounter one another CyberCindy wants to trust her, even though she is a stranger. Embarrassed by this, CyberCindy looks down at her belt for quick relief from her desire, and is pleased to note that two other cyber travellers are nearby, although they are not contactable. She looks up, feeling slightly more confident.

'Hi!', she offers.

The Samaritan woman returns, 'Hi,' the bright eyes brim confidently, and the woman carries with her the air of someone with attitude, 'How can I help you?'

green

'Well,' CyberCindy began, blurting the words out, 'for a start we want to know what Jesus looks like. We can't see his face at all – this is such a rubbish set up!'

'You'll find out what he looks like for yourself, one day,' she replies, and then adds, 'Maybe. I'm not at liberty to divulge such things. His appearance is immaterial to his nature. I would have thought you should concern yourself more with Jesus' character than his looks. You can get to know him through the Bible, you know.'

There is an awkward pause. CyberCindy feels rebuked, but then the woman suggests, 'Shall we sit down? The disciples have moved away now.'

The disciples had followed the villagers into the village, and the shade under the tree is vacant and inviting. CyberCindy, Ruth and the Samaritan Woman sit down under the shade of the olive tree.

CyberCindy turns to the woman and starts accusingly, 'Why wouldn't you give Jesus a drink?' She wanted to add, 'you old cow,' but wasn't sure that this avatar would take kindly to her abuse, which Toby was well used to.

The woman smiles softly, unperturbed by CyberCindy's aggression, nodding her head understandingly. She settles her hands in her lap, her thumbs rotating around each other, first slowly, then fast, then pausing for a moment, as she gathers breath while reflecting on the best thing to say.

She begins, 'He shouldn't have asked me.' She smiles again, 'First of all, Jews and Samaritans have hated each other for centuries. Secondly, I am a woman. Thirdly, Jesus is a holy man and I am, in the eyes of Jewish holy men, the scum of the earth. It is improper for a man to speak to a woman in public. Jesus, the Jewish Rabbi, should have known not to ask me, a Samaritan woman, for a drink. Jews think that Samaritan vessels – crockery, china, and so on – are unclean, and that they will become unclean if they use the same ones as us. They despise us. They think they are so HOLY!'

The woman pauses, and gently tugs at a thread on the hem of her skirt. 'It all stretches back, long, long ago, to the days after the Babylonian exile.' The woman's voice was deep and guttural, with an attractive twang to it, which made it difficult for CyberCindy to decipher easily.

'This area, between Judea and Galilee, was first called Samaria after the division of the kingdom. King Omri named the new capital of the northern kingdom, which he fortified, 'Samaria'. Then, some years later, between 722–721 BC, the Assyrians captured Samaria and deported Israelites of standing, in keeping with the usual practices of war in those days.'

CyberCindy is listening, but she is impatient. She hadn't asked for a history lesson, and cannot fathom why the woman is answering her in this way when all she wants to know is what made the woman refuse to give Jesus a drink. (It seemed so mean, so ungenerous.)

'Then the Assyrians settled the land with foreigners, who intermarried with the surviving Israelites. When the deported Israelites returned after the exile, they despised those Israelites who had remained and intermarried so much that they refused our offer of help to build the new

Jerusalem temple. We were scum, rubbish-heap people, heretics who couldn't be trusted.'[92]

The Samaritan woman stops for a while, pained by her words. Ruth looks enquiringly at CyberCindy, trying to monitor whether she is interested.

'Go on,' CyberCindy says lying down on the grass, as if in submission, 'I am listening, even though I haven't the foggiest what you are talking about. I hope you're going to answer my question soon.'

Putting her hands behind her head, she breaths in the hot air, waiting to listen to the undulations of the Samaritan woman's words again. But suddenly she finds herself, not in restful relaxation, but hurtling with great speed through different, alien, territory. She passes at high speed through a medley of mountainous images, her body tossed this way and that as the dark peaks loom menacingly towards her before passing by. Her head is dragged through the mountain, ominous rocks hurtling towards her, past her, through her, then suddenly she encounters a multitude of leering faces, peering at her, lips of different shapes and sizes exposing teeth in various stages of decay, eyes beaming, faces whizzing towards her, away from her, around her, above and below her.

Her body jumps involuntarily in alarm flinching uncontrollably. The sound of laughter suddenly echoes and vibrates around her, until she is not sure whether it is laughter or crying, and through the nightmare noise she discerns the sound of babies crying, and water splashing. She feels dizzy, out of control, afraid. Her body is being jogged and jolted into a different kind of virtual reality.

But even as she collides into and through unknown worlds, CyberCindy realises that when she lifted her arms to place her hands behind her head, pointing them upwards, she was giving the command to the fibre-optic network woven around her body to exit her surroundings at great speed. This is an emergency option, given as an alternative to escape from a world should other cybernauts, sharing your environment, become pests or in some way threaten the security of the system. Although she can lift the visor on her SceneSensa at any time and return to the real world, cybernauts sharing the same virtual world would have direct access to her home address, which she may not wish to disclose. The fast-track exit means that others are unable to track identity, scrambling any route by which a cybernaut might have arrived or departed. The experience is thoroughly unpleasant because CyberCindy was unprepared for it.

Once she realises what is happening, CyberCindy slowly returns her arms to her side, and as she comes to a halt looks about as she regains her balance. She witnesses a forest of frozen trees, a magical landscape. It is chilly, and she notices her breath blowing mist into the air. She consults her routemaster gopher, and is pleased to note that there is an easy route back to Sychar. Her main concern is whether Ruth will still be there. She fears her action may have caused the system to crash, and as she taps in the route to return to Sychar, she wonders what will have happened to Ruth and the Samaritan woman.

CyberCindy has to wait whilst her command is accepted; she finds the wait somehow humiliating and becomes irritable, feeling vulnerable and rather stupid. But before very long, she is careering through soft clouds and kind colours, and returns to the scene she left, to discover that Ruth is still there, as if waiting for her, even though she looks a little unkempt. Wisps of hair fall about Ruth's face; her black shawl needs adjusting for it is lopsided on her shoulders. There is an air of confusion in Ruth's eyes. But she says nothing, and gently rearranges her hair and her shawl whilst listening to the Samaritan woman, who does not acknowledge the unexpected interruption that CyberCindy has just experienced, but continues with her explanation, determinedly weaving a portrait of times past.

'Around about 400 BC the Samaritans built a temple on Mount Gerizim, in direct opposition to the Jerusalem temple. This was anathema to the Jews, for the Temple was the focus of all that they believe, the focus of their sacrificial system and their worship. In 108 BC the Hasmonaean ruler John Hyrcanus destroyed it, adding fuel to the fire of hatred between Samaritans and Jews.'

The air was still, and in the distance a dog barked. CyberCindy wondered what an Hasmonaean ruler was, but she didn't like to reveal her ignorance, as the Samaritan woman seemed to have assumed that CyberCindy was grounded in a good general knowledge. She doesn't like to disappoint her and keeps silent accordingly.

yellow

'You see, CyberCindy, we have a very strange sort of a relationship with the Jews. We have common ancestors and a common heritage. But we only take the Pentateuch as our Scriptures and disregard all those other books you find in the Jewish Scriptures.'

'What, like Ruth?', CyberCindy asks.

The Samaritan woman casts a quick look towards Ruth, and then turns back to CyberCindy.

'Yes, like Ruth', she answers calmly.

Ruth turns her head away, but says nothing.

The woman continues, 'These days Samaria has no separate political existence from Judea, for both regions are united under the Roman procurator. Samaria is defined by its history and religion. Some travellers so hate us they will avoid coming through the area, preferring to cross the Jordan near Jericho, travel north up the east bank, going through Gentile territory – yes, Gentile territory – crossing back to the west bank near the Lake of Galilee.

> ? *Jews viewed the Samaritans not only as the children of political rebels, but as racial half-breeds whose religion was tainted by various unacceptable elements.*[93] *Once we can appreciate this, we can not only sympathise with the woman's reaction, but begin to grasp the enormity and breadth of Jesus' ministry – that he came to bring salvation to all, regardless of ethnic background and religious*

belief. God's agenda for the world is reconciliation; that his people may be reconciled to himself and then to one another.

They want to be seen to have nothing to do with us at all. You see, because the Jews rejected us long ago, we focus our worship not on Jerusalem but on Mount Gerizim.'

The woman gazed across to the mountain on her right. It was large and majestic, looming up from the countryside almost ominously.

'I think the temple on Mount Gerizim brings just as much glory to God as the one in Jerusalem. And as the Jews excluded us, we have every right to worship where we like. And I am not going to have anyone telling me that they are better than us, because they're not. In fact, I would rather be a Samaritan than anything else. We obey the Law, we love God, and we're religiously righteous. At least,' she pauses, 'that's what I thought ... before I ... met ... Jesus.'

The sheep bleat in the distance, and CyberCindy suddenly remembers that she was due to meet Australian Michael at Heathrow Airport that day, at 17:00 hrs. She turns a knob on her visor, and is instantly able to lift it up, holding her existence in the virtual world of Sychar whilst checking the time by the clock in her flat. (She could have opted for a digital clock to be displayed whilst travelling in virtual reality, but she finds this distracting.) It is only 14:20 hrs. She has plenty more time. She puts her SceneSensa back over her head and returns to her female friends.

'Well, speaking as one who was not excluded by the Israelites, but included into their community against all the odds, and not just included, but clearly a part of God's purposes for salvation, can I just say that my experience has been completely different from yours.' Ruth the Moabite interjects, addressing the Samaritan woman. CyberCindy sits alert. This is going to be interesting.

'Ruth, please don't misunderstand me,' the Samaritan woman responds, 'I know that I am included in the family of God beyond any reasonable doubt, now that I have met the Messiah for myself. But tell me, what made you commit yourself to the Israelites? Weren't Moabites a hated race, just like the Samaritans? And you didn't have my advantage, did you? As an ancestor of King David, you didn't even have the prospect of a Messiah to look forward to.'

'Yes, you know we were cursed, and so does CyberCindy. But it seems to be that individuals are not bound to conform to their collective groupings. It is the duty of each and every person on earth to account for his or her life before God. It is unethical to say that you can justify your actions because you are one of a people. Everyone has to justify their actions because they will stand before God on judgement day. And as believers it is one of our responsibilities to make that judgement known.' Ruth and the Samaritan woman both instinctively turn towards CyberCindy, who in her imagination has begun to picture herself skating on an ice rink with points being awarded out of ten. Ruth continues, 'For me, faith is all about commitment, commitment to God and his people and to lasting relationships.'

The Samaritan woman smiles, 'For me, faith is all about knowing Jesus. What about you, CyberCindy?'

'Me?', CyberCindy, who is surprised to be asked, 'Faith? I dunno. I think faith is all about being true to yourself.'

As CyberCindy speaks, it seems to her that the women fade in colour, and the scene in which she is ensconced flickers a little, almost as if there has been a power cut. She decides the time has come for a walk, and gets up, moving away from the women. 'I'm just going for a walk,' she murmurs, and leaving the women behind her, walks towards the well.

CyberCindy peers over the edge and looks down, surprised to discover that she can see the water in it. She picks up a little stone and drops it. Plop! She glances over to the tree. The women are sitting quietly, apparently admiring the view. CyberCindy looks around too, and takes in the great panorama of undulating hills, the sun warm on her face. After a while, she returns to the women with purposeful strides, and as she approaches asks in a tone of urgent enquiry,

'Yes, but where are you both now? I mean, how do you categorise yourselves? Are you both Christians, or what?', she asks impetuously.

The question hangs in the air and the Samaritan woman and Ruth exchange looks, cautiously at first, but then rising to a smile.

'Yes, CyberCindy, we're both Christians,' they say together.

? *It may be simplistic or technically inaccurate to claim that Ruth is a Christian, in that she lived pre-Christ. As a character in the Old Testament who sought to be faithful to God, Ruth is incorporated into God's family which transcends aspects of time. Ruth's wholehearted commitment to*

145

> *God, which can only be measured on the revelation*
> *that God had given to his people at that point in*
> *time, secures salvation for her.*

'Oh, boy!', CyberCindy murmurs, in a non-threatening way. It is giving her pleasure to sit with people who in normal space and time were born thousands of centuries apart. For the first time in her cyberspace travels, CyberCindy consciously admires the women, and wishes they were real. She admires the Samaritan woman and her knowledge, her enthusiasm. She looks at Ruth's deep eyes, her well-defined face, and waits to hear the familiar soft authority of Ruth's voice once again, recognising the nuances of her mouth that indicate that she is about to say something.

'Do you know, CyberCindy, that Sychar is probably what is known in the twenty-first century as the little village of Askar, on the shoulder of Mount Ebal, opposite Mount Gerizim?', Ruth asks.

'Oh, really?', CyberCindy responds. The tone of her words reveals that she is evidently unimpressed. She may admire the women, but she is not going to have them brainwash her.

blue

'Everyone knows that Jacob's well is very near the plot of ground Jacob gave to his son Joseph, as recorded in Genesis 48:22,' Ruth continues, 'When the Israelites first conquered and settled in Canaan, they buried the bones of Joseph, near here, at Shechem, in the tract of land that Jacob bought for a hundred pieces of silver from the sons of Hamor, the father of Shechem.' Ruth pauses, and then adds, 'I believe Shechem is known as Balata these days, and if you were to go there in person, CyberCindy, you would find Joseph's tomb a few hundred yards north-west of Jacob's well.'

'Hmm,' CyberCindy offered, 'Thanks for the holiday update.'

The women stare at CyberCindy blankly, unsure of her meaning. She continues with a question, 'So you mean Sychar is a real place?'

The Samaritan woman responds quickly, 'Of course it is a real place!'

Ruth interjects, 'Whatever made you think it might not be?'

'Well, I was just wondering the other day who put your story to paper.'

The Samaritan woman looks towards Ruth, shifting her buttocks on the grass, and snatches at a long blade, tearing it apart.

'And without wishing to be offensive,' CyberCindy continues, this time addressing the Samaritan woman,

'Who was at the well to know and write down what Jesus said to you and what you said back to him? It seems logical to me that most of your stories are made up. They have to be. Someone created the words in the book just as someone created this virtual world. The Bible can only ever be a sort of news documentary on the Truth, can't it, I mean it can't possibly be Truth, because someone wrote it with their own subjective bias.'

? *Fairytales, myths and legends all have their part to play in forging norms of good and evil.*

Ruth does not know how to reply, and the Samaritan woman looks away, in anger, gathering her thoughts.

'It's OK,' CyberCindy comments reassuringly, 'it doesn't matter whether it happened like it says, does it? I mean, what matters is what it says, isn't it?'

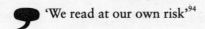 'We read at our own risk'[94]

Before Ruth could construct an adequate reply, the Samaritan woman interjects, 'I can assure you that I am a real person!'

CyberCindy is not convinced, 'I'm not bothered whether you're real or fictitious, my point is that just because the Bible mentions a definite place, which we can still visit today,' she turns to the woman and goes off at a tangent, 'and incidentally, I wonder what you think about being included in the Christian Scriptures when you reject most of the Hebrew ones,' and not waiting for a reply, turns back to Ruth, 'that doesn't prove that it really happened, does it? I could tell a story all about someone living in Threadneedle Street in London, but that doesn't mean

148

the story is true. Except, of course, if I tell the story to you, then the story becomes a real part of your life and experience doesn't it? I mean, when we cry about a film, or TV soaps, the tears are still real tears aren't they? They're not pretend, just because the characters are actors. When the nation grieved the death of Princess Diana it was real grief even though 99 per cent of the population had never met her. Wasn't it? So why does it matter if your story is true or not? If I read the book it's a part of me, if I don't, then it isn't. Why not just be happy with a good story. Why do you biblical types insist on rooting everything in history, or geography? What's wrong with experience?'

? *Culpepper spearheaded narrative criticism, arguing that the 'real issue is whether 'his story' can be true if it is not 'history' ... As long as readers require the Gospel to be a window on the ministry of Jesus before they will see truth in it, accepting the Gospel will mean believing that the story it tells corresponds exactly to what actually happened during Jesus' ministry.'[95] While this may be a necessary corrective to a literalist understanding of the text which may overlook context, an approach to Scripture which denies its historicity is limited in scope and potential, for it muddles fact with fiction, and meaning may be obscured rather than clarified. Stibbe takes issue with Culpepper for neglecting historical features within the Fourth Gospel, and treating the final form as an 'autonomous narrative world', with no consideration of historicity and argues that John used his 'historical imagination' in compiling his Gospel.[96]*

149

As neither the author nor the original recipients are available today, it is only by means of the written text itself that the most likely meaning can be reconstructed. Schneiders argues that a strictly historical approach to the New Testament is limited in value, for she sees it as primarily religious literature whose purpose is 'to bear witness to the faith of the first Christians and thereby to enlighten the faith understanding of the reader in such a way as to challenge him or her to ongoing conversion and increased fidelity in Christ'.[97] Collingwood claims that it is nonsense to maintain that 'a truthful historical account is one in which the historian merely reproduces the ready-made statements of his authorities'.[98] Biblical writers have been obliged to order their material in a certain way. If the presentation of the text is ignored, the underlying truth(s) of a passage may be overlooked, or do little justice to the God-given text. O'Day argues that 'the narrative does not mediate the revelation but is the revelation' conforming to the great postmodern sound bite that 'the medium is the message'.[99] She is thus giving weight to the narrative that traditional Christianity gives to the role of the Holy Spirit.[100]

Historical exegesis is essential to biblical hermeneutics because it roots and grounds God's redemption in reality. Once exegetes begin to question the actuality of the events described as historical, then faith becomes a matter of personal opinion and salvation a question of one's perspective, rather than God's saving acts. The beauty of the gospel is that God has intervened in the world; that he has dealt with sin and that he desires a full relationship with his people.

Without a historical understanding of first-century culture, we may be making hermeneutical jumps and leaps that cannot be justified. Whilst this is inevitable to a certain degree, for we cannot know precisely, if the Bible is not read in context, it is easy to misunderstand its message. Is Jesus the Saviour of the world in actuality or only in the figment of the Gospel writer's imagination? Having said that, it does not follow that just because an event is presented as 'story' it is fabrication – after all, anyone who reads newspapers or watches television news will have an understanding that the presentation is subject to edits and subjective decisions on what is and what is not important.

(Exegete: interpreter, scholar.)

(Hermeneutics: the study of methods of biblical interpretation.)

'Because, CyberCindy, Jesus' ministry on earth was the pinnacle of time,' Ruth replies reassuringly, beaming a persuasive smile, 'Besides which, the author does claim to be reporting history, and it would be an injustice to ignore that fact! Indeed, most of the events reported throughout the Gospel are rooted in time and geography.'[101]

This is the disciple who testifies to these things and who wrote them down. We know that his testimony is true. Jesus did many other things as well. If every one of them were written down, I suppose that even the whole world would not have room for the books that would be written (John 21:24–25).

The Samaritan woman, however, takes umbrage, 'If you are suggesting for one moment that I am a figment of someone's imagination you are very much mistaken, CyberCindy,' she says passionately, 'Jesus really is the Messiah and he has already changed my whole life. Some ignorant people like to think that I am some sort of symbolic figure, a cardboard cut-out invented by the author simply to achieve her – or his – own ends. And whilst that may be intriguing to some, it hardly reflects reality.'

CyberCindy is unperturbed. 'Changed your life? What, in a day?', she queries, 'How?'

'God loves me. That changes everything. You don't think I would have come over here to talk to you two, do you, if something momentous hadn't happened inside me.

Ruth is a proselyte; she has converted to Judaism. Naturally, I would despise her, have nothing to do with her. She has taken on board all the Israelite teaching; she loves the people I naturally loathed. She has even rejected her own people to be accepted amongst the Israelites. And before today, I would have said she was a fool. Her son will be a half-cast, just like we Samaritans were regarded as impure half-casts of our ancestors. Of course, the big joke is that Ruth's great grandchild ends up being King of Israel. So it would seem that racial purity isn't such a hot issue after all, in God's eyes. God's purposes for salvation go way beyond exclusive little coteries.'

? *Whilst Old Testament ideology is nearly always negative in its view of foreign women, ironically, the Old Testament is also littered with accounts of royal marriages to foreigners; other prominent leaders also intermarry.*[102] *It seems then* *that foreign women were accepted whole-heartedly into the community when they adopted the systems of values and beliefs of their husband's environment. When a woman continued to practise foreign ways after her marriage, she and her children were subject to disapproval. The biblical expectation seems to be that of conversion and acceptance or non-conversion and rejection.*

The Samaritan woman continues, 'Jesus took me seriously. For a start, he set aside convention and spoke to me.'

? *Some ancient Jewish literature advises against public conversation of a man with a woman, stating that 'He that talks much with womankind brings evil upon himself' (m. Pike Aboth 1:5) and 'It is forbidden to give a woman any greeting' (b. Kiddushim 70a). There are also texts which warn against Jewish contact with Samaritans for 'The daughters of Samaria are deemed unclean as menstruants from their cradle.' (M. Niddah 4:1).[103] Maccini argues that 'Samaritan dispositions toward women became increasingly subordinationist only with time, particularly under Muslim influence'.[104]*

yellow

'Yes,' Ruth adds 'It's strange isn't it, that some scholars think that I was written after the exiles returned, as a response to Nehemiah's and Ezra's call to marital purity, in order to argue, contrary to their teaching, that intermarriage was no bad thing. But I don't think that's why I was written. As I have said before, the theme of my book is redemption from beginning to end. God's heart is certainly for the oppressed, the marginalised. (Only because, of course, they are oppressed and marginalised, not because he likes injustice!) God is love. He calls his people to love. Love is costly and most of us prefer following our own whims and fancies, justifying our own disobedience to Yahweh through clever manipulation of the Scriptures, or easier still, by ignoring them.'

? *Historical-critical exegesis can elevate the preacher to a privileged position of control; the presupposition is that 'ordinary readers' are not in a position to accurately discern the message of the text, for they do not possess the privileged information accessed by the researcher/ teacher. There is a relationship of teacher/taught which, if wrongly applied, could lead to dictator/ vulnerable, which, if wrongly applied could lead to misleader/misled. Whilst seeking objectivity, if exegetes fail to take into account their 'interested character' they will almost certainly contain* *subjective elements, which are not recognised as such.*[105]

All biblical scholarship is vulnerable; all scholars will subconsciously or consciously promote their own theological assumptions. Schussler Fiorenza is understandably keen to expose biblical scholarship 'which "renders God" a 'God of patriarchal oppression'.[106] *Believing that God is essentially good, Kroeger and Evans rightly argue that view that the Scriptures are meant for healing rather than hurt, for affirmation of all persons, especially those who are oppressed.*[107]

In our endeavour to seek out truth, we need to clear ourselves of rubble, so that God has a clear highway on which to travel, and yet it is impossible to be purely objective.

'You are right, Ruth,' the Samaritan woman adds, 'but let me make one thing very clear. Jesus won my heart by meeting me where I was. First of all he took me by surprise, breaking the barriers of religious etiquette. Of course, I was affronted at first and thought him very rude. But because he challenged my assumptions, we began to talk about things close to my heart which I have hardly ever spoken about to anyone else apart from fellow Samaritans. And when we talked, he provoked me,[108] challenged me,[109] forced me to face up to reality,[110] and yet, miraculously, at the same time he gave me hope, and a reason for living.'[111]

> ❞ Theologians today are being forced to 'relinquish their understanding of the Bible as a 'classic' and to develop a critical hermeneutics rather than a 'hermeneutics of consent'.[112]

'Hope?', CyberCindy queries, 'Ruth, you said you would give me hope, if I remember rightly.'

'And have I?', Ruth asks.

'No!', CyberCindy says simply, 'But that's because I think hope is unrealistic. My generation is, underneath all the glitz, depressed, really. We are the children of divorce, broken relationships. My father died of AIDS, and I am out of touch with my mother. So today is what counts, because the past has let me down and the future is uncertain. Unlike you,' she says, turning to the Samaritan woman, 'I'm not hanging around for a Messiah. I don't even know what a Messiah is. I really can't get your drift.'

> *The world is suspicious of the evangelical message of certainty. The Christian life has many unanswered questions, unsolved problems, and many ongoing struggles with belief. But Christians can proclaim the power of the resurrection, and they can have fellowship in Christ's suffering as they engage with people in the world who are, in varying degrees, broken and just like them.*

'Jesus is the source of life,' the Samaritan woman states.

'But he is just a person, he's not an answer,' retorts CyberCindy.

'A very special person,' adds Ruth.

'A very, very special person,' the Samaritan woman adds almost dreamily.

'Do you think he's special just because he knew how many husbands you had? Haven't you ever come across a clairvoyant before?', CyberCindy enquired accusingly.

'Jesus is not a clairvoyant, you foolish woman,' the woman replied, 'although I do think it's amazing that he knows me.'

'Knows about you!', corrected CyberCindy, 'And don't call me woman.'

'No, knows me. He knows me. And he knows everything about me.' The woman looked over to the village, as if pining for him.

'Is it true that you've had five husbands?', CyberCindy asks abruptly.

'Yes,' the Samaritan woman replies, 'Men these days are simply useless at sticking at relationships. They think I am a commodity, like their land or cattle. When they decide I am not what they want they divorce me. Then they find someone younger and prettier, who'll produce for them the baby boys that I can't.' The woman pauses, resignedly, 'Or they die on you, leaving their brothers to marry you.' She tugs at a blade of grass again, 'Without a man, CyberCindy, you're just a nobody and you have no security and no means of finding any.'

'That's nonsense!', CyberCindy exclaimed heatedly, 'Of course you're a somebody! Everyone has value. Why don't you just get a job if you want your independence?'

Ruth interrupts, 'CyberCindy, I've already tried to explain to you. In a patriarchal society women are like a second sex; good for having babies and running the home; giving stability and order to society, but not given the opportunity to exercise their many other God-given gifts. Most commentators seem to think that the Samaritan woman was a prostitute, or at least a woman of low morals. It doesn't even occur to them that she has no rights at all. She is not able to divorce her husbands, because the law only permits men to divorce their wives.'

> **?** *Mark 10:2 indicates that the issue of divorce was one on the contemporary theological agenda. There were basically two schools of thought on the issue in Jesus' day – those who followed the teaching of Shammai who interpreted the 'something indecent' in Deuteronomy 24:1 as being a sexual offence, and those who followed Hillel, who claimed that 'becomes displeasing' could incorporate the most trivial action which caused irritation to the husband.*[113]

'As you have seen yourself, our friend here has the respect of all the villagers, and she is pretty intelligent too, arguing with Jesus mostly on theological grounds. I wouldn't be at all surprised if she told us she was a prophetess.'

> **?** *The text itself is clear evidence that the woman, far from being inarticulate or ignorant, has a sound grasp of the theological issues of the day. Carson, in contrasting the woman with the religious leader Nicodemus (John 3) asserts that she was 'unschooled, without influence, despised and capable only of folk religion'.*[114] *If she were unschooled she would not engage in theological debate with a Rabbi, if she had no influence she would not have been able to persuade the villagers to examine Jesus for themselves. There is nothing in the text to warrant the assertion that she was despised, except that she goes to the well alone. The reference to folk religion is undoubtedly offensive*

to Samaritans, who would not view themselves in this way.

> Because Samaritans interpreted the Pentateuch strictly, the injunction of Deuteronomy 31:12 indicates that their practice of educating children of both sexes in the law and Samaritan traditions is not an innovation but probably dates back to their origins.[115]

'Well?', CyberCindy asks the woman.

'Well what?'.

'Are you a prophetess?'

'What do you think, CyberCindy?'

'I s'pose it's possible,' CyberCindy replies.

? *Some ancient texts claim that 'providing one's daughters with a knowledge of the Torah was as inappropriate as teaching them lechery'.[116] Whilst we may (justifiably) be dismayed at such an attitude, the twentieth century is no panacea for women. Storkey pointed out in 1985 that there is still widespread injustice to women in our society – in family life, education, the law, the Church and marriage. Years on and women are still not respected as men's equals. The proportion of women in leadership roles is small, even though there are more women in responsible positions in parliament, the church and society at large today. 'The patriarchal emphasis of our society means that the unjust way many men behave towards women is legitimated in legal and economic structures. It is embedded in attitudes and stereotypes.'[117] Everyone is the loser whilst this continues; men lose out on their God-given fathering role whilst they pursue lucrative careers; women bear the exclusive brunt of child rearing. Whilst these trends are changing, shared parenting is nowhere near normative. Nowhere does the Bible dictate that the female role should be in the home and the male role should be in work. Work is the biblical model for all; and fathers and mothers are both called to be actively engaged in the bringing up of children.*

'But would a prophetess marry five times?', CyberCindy queried, pleased that she had at last been able to enter into something of the woman's experience.

'She would if some of her husbands had divorced her and others had died on her,' the woman said sadly.

red

CyberCindy has had enough of this discussion. She has become bored; the conversation is too serious and she doesn't wish to discuss death. It is time to go.

'C'mon Ruth, we're going home.'

'CyberCindy, that's not fair! I haven't seen Jesus yet!', Ruth protests.

'Oh, we'll come again another time. I've had enough of this history lesson. Besides, I have a friend to meet,' and then she adds, spitefully, as an afterthought, 'Someone real.'

CyberCindy is frustrated that the people whose company she finds most compelling are cyber-world creations. A longing has surfaced for real company, real relationships. Ironically, she still vents her anger on these fictional characters; because she is actively interacting with them. To spite an avatar is ludicrous; but virtual reality is beginning to get under her skin.

Without more ado, she taps the light on her belt, and suddenly, strangely, CyberCindy is transported through other worlds, Ruth sitting statuesque and still beside her as together they traverse through cyberspace, her gaze haunting and silent. They arrive at the virtual world of Ruth quickly, and CyberCindy unlinks Ruth, unhooking her from the transmitter, dumping her in her Old Testament world, and flies home at high speed, fast-forwarding straight through Gibson. Once home, CyberCindy is conscious of a dull ache in her legs, for she has been in cyberspace for over three hours. Code laws recommend a maximum of two.

Australian Michael had short black hair highlighted with red streaks, his long thin face a perfect setting for the little round spectacles which glittered in the light, and balanced precariously half way down his long nose, allowing light blue eyes to scan the world over the top of their rim. CyberCindy thought him rather attractive.

'Hi!', she beamed.

'Hi!', he beamed back.

Later that evening, after a very pleasant meal, the talk gravitates to things spiritual. CyberCindy wants to get some insight on Australian Michael's spirituality, and she wants to talk to someone about her adventures in cyberspace. But as soon as she begins telling Australian Michael how she has 'hit' on Christianity, he interrupts her to ask if she believes in reincarnation. CyberCindy isn't sure whether she believes in reincarnation. She thinks it is feasible.

'Well, I have proof,' Australian Michael announces, 'I have a magazine back home which has on its front cover a photograph of a moth. And if you get a magnifying glass, and put it on top of the head, you will see, clear as daylight, a man's face. You can see his eyes and his nose and his mouth, well he's shouting about something. No doubt about it. It's the most graphic evidence I've ever come across.'

Australian Michael's manner is that of sharing a secret which he had chosen to divulge to CyberCindy because she was an intimate friend.

Australian Michael is an intelligent man. He is interested in a great many things and knowledgeable about most of them. He has an ambiguous past, which CyberCindy takes to mean he possibly has children, and he likes to keep abreast of what is going on in the world.

At his disclosure, CyberCindy has an irrepressible urge to laugh. She gazes at Australian Michael over the wine bottle on the table, and whilst she feels distanced from him, she gains in inner confidence. If he believes that, then maybe belief in Jesus isn't quite so strange.

Later that week, CyberCindy says goodbye to Australian Michael, and after she sees him off at the station, she returns to her flat in melancholy mood to find a small brown envelope stuck in the letterbox. There is no indication who it is from, no note, no postmark, no nothing. She very rarely received letters or parcels, and the little package intrigues her. When she opens it she finds it to be a little book entitled *The Story of Emma B. Lever* by Gill Rowell. CyberCindy reads it immediately, conscious of a general lethargy because Michael has gone.

This is the story of Emma B. Lever, who one summery day skipped to market, skippetty-hoppity, skippetty-hoppity, singing,

> 'God's not dead, no! He is alive!
> Serve him with my hands (clap, clap),
> Follow with my feet (stamp, stamp),
> Love Him in my heart (boom, boom),
> Know Him in my life (whoosh!)
> For He's alive in me!'[118]

When she arrived at market, however, she came across a Madman, much distressed, with a lantern in his hand, surrounded by silent on-lookers, crying out: 'God is dead. God remains dead. And we have killed him. How shall we, the murderers of all murders, comfort ourselves?' (Nietzsche). The Madman issued forth relentlessly, and Emma B. Lever could not bear to hear it. She was much upset by his words, and when he threw his lantern to the ground, and it broke, and went out, she went to church in great anguish to pray. After a time, who should enter but the Madman himself, full of angst, who sang a sad song and then cried out from the depths of his belly, 'What are these churches now if they are not the tombs and sepulchres of God?' (Nietzsche).

Emma decided to confront him, 'Excuse me, kind sir, but I fear for you, for I know that God is alive, and that, yea, though we killed him, He rose again.'

The Madman laughed piteously at the young girl, 'Prove it, my little one, prove it!' There was something in his voice that made Emma think he was the loneliest man that ever existed.

'I fear to attempt to do so, for I know that there is no one proof or even group of proofs which will satisfy you; all I can do is show you reasonable theories ... my fear is that you are an unreasonable man.'

'You may be right in your assessment,' said he, 'but what does that matter to me?'

'Well, perhaps if you could spare the time, I could at least try,' and her heart missed a beat as she spoke, for she was afraid that this God whom she knew to be alive might be proved to be dead after all.

'I have time, for I came too early,' the Madman confessed, and he looked at Emma out of the corner of his eye and thought, 'You are absurd, and yet you are there' (Sartre).

'You will have to bear with me,' Emma said, 'for I know that you believe we have lost all objective truth. And yet, if that is so, I would rather be dead.'

The Madman was pleased. 'There is but one philosophical option,' he remembered, 'and that is suicide' (Camus).

'Can you imagine that than which nothing greater can be conceived?', Emma B. Lever began.

'I think I might,' he replied, 'after all, I am a fool.'

'Do you agree that something that would be greater than that which can be conceived would be actual?'

'Indeed.'

'If, then, that than which nothing greater can be conceived is true to its name and description then it must exist both in the mind and in reality ... therefore ... God must exist!', she said happily, adding, 'Good old Abbot Anselm!' (For it was his theory that she was expounding.)

At that point Emma and the Madman found themselves miraculously transported to Gaunilo's Island, which was a very beautiful island. The Madman looked about him, amazed. ('Am I in heaven?' he wondered, though he dare not ask.) He turned to Emma.

'This is perfection. This is that than which nothing greater can be conceived! ... There could be nothing greater than this!', he proclaimed.

Emma knew that the island was not God, although it did seem to reveal something to her about God.

It was then that she remembered Aquinas' five ways to God, and although this is based on empirical presuppositions that our senses are reliable, which she was sure the Madman would reject, she thought it to be a good starting point (Aquinas).

'Sir,' she began, 'take a look at that bird of paradise on yonder coconut tree.' The Madman looked. 'Where did it come from? Why, it came from an egg of a bird of paradise. And where did that bird of paradise come from? Why, from an egg of a bird of paradise. But, if we regress back in the chain of cause, I think you will have to agree with me that ultimately there must have first existed something that came from nothing. This is what people call God.' The Madman was silent. Emma went on. 'Or take those monkeys over there. Why do they move? What causes them to move? Well, any manner of things, but ultimately, if we regress back in the chain of cause, I am sure you will agree with me that there was first something which caused them to move and this was in itself an unmoved mover. This is what people call God.'

'Your argument, although purporting to be logical, is quite illogical,' the Madman retorted, 'You have moved from the experience of the finite and mortal to what is infinite and immortal without any explanation whatsoever! You have some strange notion that this world has some sort of coherence, or order, and that immanence and transcendence can be linked. Truth is not there to be discovered! Truth is to be created! You are looking backward when you should be looking forward!'

Just at that point a savage walked by gazing intently at a watch, muttering words of marvel and awe to himself, 'Where diz vrom, who mek it?'

'William Paley's watch!', thought Emma, and she launched forth once more.

'Look at yonder savage,' she began. The Madman looked. 'See how he marvels at the watch, he is aware, is he not, that the watch is the result of the work of an intelligent mind. And yet he has never seen a watch before. And even if the watch has stopped functioning, he will still know that it has been made, that it didn't just happen. And look about this island! Isn't it manifestly designed, isn't it perfectly formed, I mean, surely, you must agree that there has to be a designer and orderer of the universe, and that this is what people know to be God?' The Madman was unimpressed. 'If God created this beautiful island, then tell me, child, did he create that savage savage?'

The savage had taken a knife to his wrists, and was licking his lips on the blood that flowed from them in masochistic glee.

'Oh no!', Emma cried, 'We must do something to stop him!'

'Why interfere? Leave him alone to embrace his own death, its his life: let him experience the final symbol of his absurdity in peace,' rebuked the Madman, 'He has made his own choice, untainted by you and your morals, good luck to him, I say!'

'No!', Emma shrieked, 'No, what he is doing is wrong!'

'Wrong? Wrong? Have you not heard what I have been saying, my dear? We have lost God therefore we have lost everything! There is no right; there is no wrong. If there is no God, everything is permitted! [Dostoyevsky] Face up to reality: let the savage answer his own life's apparent meaninglessness and despair. Man is nothing else but that which he makes himself. Let him experience the great negation authentically.'

Emma was flabbergasted. Never before had she come across such blatant immorality. She had always believed she owned some sort of conscience, invisible to the phenomenological world, which stemmed from the supernatural and divine realm of God. And she remembered what Kant had said, that the heart of morality is to do the right thing for its own sake, and yet she knew that doing right because it was right was not always rewarded in this life (Kant). She looked at the grey, bleak figure of the Madman and realised that somehow he would never accept that immortality and life beyond the grave would allow time for the rewarding of virtue and the punishment of evil, or that the very existence of morality in the world is an indicator pointing to the existence of God. To someone who claims that God is dead, life is certainly meaningless, meaningless, utterly meaningless.

'No wonder he thinks he has to create truth, poor fool!', she thought.

'This island does not exist,' the Madman stated abruptly, 'It is an illusion, like God. This island is a figment of our imagination; it's not real, how could it be – we were in the church a moment ago.'

'Perhaps we ought to go home,' Emma retorted, 'but before we do, let me just say this: this island isn't perfect because I can imagine a more perfect island than this, more birds of paradise, more monkeys, more colours, more everything. God's existence is absolutely perfect and cannot be likened to the existence of so-called perfect islands; it is only of God that we can say it is greater to exist than not to exist. God must necessarily exist, or he would not be God at all. And what is more, when you say God is dead, you are talking nonsense. How can God be God and be dead? To talk of God at all is to talk of him existing, for God is self-existent, he is omnipotent and omniscient.'

'Pah! Take me home: the twenty-first century is here, and my time is nigh! God is dead, he is dead, I tell you, and we have killed him.'

Emma B. Lever and the Madman found themselves back in the church. The Madman looked at Emma with dark haunting eyes heavy with sorrow, and not a little hatred, 'You see, little girl, it is impossible to prove that God is alive...objectively, or subjectively, and you are basing your life on a delusion, a lie. Pah! That would not be so bad if you kept the lie to yourself, but you are bent on incorporating others into your fantasy!' And he spat at her.

As the Madman shuffled away, Emma, depressed and defeated, focussed her attention on the empty wooden cross hanging at the front of the church. She thought of the song she had sung as she had skipped to market, 'God's not dead! No! He is alive!', and pondered on things philosophical.

'Is God only something I feel, I experience?', she asked herself. 'No,' she answered, 'no, God is much more than simply experience, although I cannot deny my own subjective knowledge of him. I know him to be alive because I experience him, yes, but I could be deluding myself. I think, overall, that if we consider all the arguments that point to the existence of God, then it is actually irrational not to accept his objective existence. There is no conclusive proof that God does not exist, after all. If he is an objective reality, and we are imperfect human beings, tainted by our limited capacities and personal subjectivities (assuming that we are not gods), then it stands to reason that we can't prove him. God told Moses "I am who I am".[119] Jesus emphasised this when he said, "Before Abraham was, I am".[120] God simply is, and He has chosen to reveal Himself to us in many wonderful and exciting ways, especially in his book, his word, the Bible. I think I would incline to believe the words of Jesus to those of Descartes, famous for his "I think, therefore I am".'

'I was lost, Lord,' Emma said aloud, speaking to her God, 'until you found me', and she remembered the haunting look of hatred in the Madman's eye. For he had hated her, not because she had been unable to prove God's existence to him, which was what he had expected in any case, but because she owned something that he had chosen not to own, and that he could not grasp. The Madman had smashed the lantern to the ground, and watched the light go out, and yet in Emma B. Lever herself he had caught a glimpse of that light, and he hated her for the joy and hope she had in her living God, a God for whom he mourned.

Emma skipped out of the church, humming to herself an old refrain that came to mind,

> 'The best book to read is the Bible,
> the best book to read is the Bible
> if you read it every day
> it will help you on your way,
> Oh, the best book to read is the Bible!'[121]

CyberCindy wondered who had put the book in her letterbox. She thinks the local nutters from the church around the corner must have delivered it. She likes the story, but puts it to one side on her desk, aware that deadlines are looming and she has little inclination to meet them. She sits still for a moment, and then turns to her computer to refresh her memory of the tasks to which she has been assigned. She has several phone calls to make, e-mails to reply to and preparation for a cyberspace presentation she is to make on a proposal to a multi-national company in Bosnia due in by the end of the week.

She resigns herself to her tasks, and sits at her desk, dials a number gazing into the audiovisual screen (the AVS), trying to look cheerful, 'Good morning, NOVI MOST International, can I help you?'

The face on the screen looks motherly, and CyberCindy's confidence is immediately boosted, for she knows the woman peering at her will perceive her to be a dynamic cyber consultant, 'Johan, please,' she says, with authority. It is good to get back to work.

Grace was in all her steps, Heav'n in her Eye,
In every gesture, dignity and love.[122]

The Samaritan woman was pleased to see CyberCindy again. 'Welcome to the well,' she greeted with a whimsical smile.

'Thanks,' CyberCindy responded and continued, not knowing if she was being sarcastic or honest, 'I've come to spiritually drink of it. Tell me, Sam, why do you think Jesus is so special?' There is a slight mocking tone to CyberCindy's voice and a demeanour of superiority, but the Samaritan woman is insensitive to early twenty-first-century nuances of intonation and appears to be delighted at the question.

? *There is a theory that having had five husbands, and currently living with a man, Jesus becomes the seventh – and therefore the perfect – man in the woman's life. Some have argued that the whole episode, written as it is, is styled in such a way as to lead the reader to expect it to conclude with a wedding, rather than the refusal of Jesus to partake of the food brought to him by the disciples. As a symbolic narrative, 'the woman of Samaria becomes the eschatological bride ... No longer is Israel alone the bride of Yahweh'.*[123] *Focussing on this perspective, the narrative becomes a documentary on Jesus' mission to all nations and the unity the gospel brings across nationalistic boundaries.*

'Jesus is the Messiah, the Saviour of the world,' the woman begins, without pausing for breath, 'In him all are set free, free from the bondage of sin.'

CyberCindy frowns.

The woman carries on, 'Free to be the people that God has created us to be, free to love, free to care. You know, CyberCindy, Jesus has joined together the boundaries that separated Jew and Samaritan. He trusted me, a woman, with saving knowledge. He has given me worth. He is not interested in exacerbating issues of race or class or gender, in issues that seek to set up one part of society as superior to another part. But he is interested in justice. And he is interested in having a relationship with his people. But his people put up barriers; they make God in their own image. We are talking mega-God here, grand God, creator God – God of everything; God of the great and the small, the world and the tiny little speck of dust in your eye. How can I tell you what Jesus is like, or why he is special? He is simply everything to me.'

The sky behind the woman's frame is clear and bright, the blue haze giving a vibrant background to the woman's soft features.

'Would it be different if he were a woman?', CyberCindy asked, 'Say, if Ruth claimed to be the Messiah, how would that fit?'

'Well, Ruth hasn't claimed to be the Messiah.'

'She told me she is a redeemer.'

'Hmm. That is interesting,' a pause … then, 'There is a sense in which all human beings are capable of fulfilling a redemptive role, but not in the way that Jesus is redeemer.'

The woman stops talking for a moment, her eyes gazing in the direction of the village, her fingers gently stroking the handle of the empty water jar resting against the well. CyberCindy has an itch on her nose. She scratches it, and immediately sneezes. She has no tissues with her, and so puts the virtual world of Sychar on hold and exits quickly, zooming home via Gibson, quickly finding herself in the sanctuary of her apartment. The box of tissues on her desk is empty. She sneezes again, and swears vociferously. She returns to the virtual world of Sychar and exits fast out of it, trying to be patient while the system allows her to exit. Once she gets the free light, she unplugs her Rompacomp, takes off her grips and SceneSensa and strides as fast as she can to the toilet, her movement mechanical and awkward.

She rips a large quantity of toilet paper off the roll and blows her nose. She tugs at the roll a second time, stuffing the soft blue paper into her belt, before deciding to take the roll off the holder completely and take it back to her desk. She doesn't wish her conversation with the Samaritan woman to be interrupted again. She is indignant at the time this unexpected excursion has wasted. She longs for the day when she will be able to insert a chip somewhere in her brain, or behind her ear, to enable her to inhabit both the actual and the virtual simultaneously, without all this cumbersome gear. But she resigns herself to its strictures, and rejoins the Samaritan woman, speeding through cyberspace on FastTrack, a shortcut which enables the cyber traveller to return at high speed and bypass the conventions of normal cyberspace travel. She presses a small flashing button on her wrist, and is able to meet the Samaritan woman just where she left her, continuing with her explanation, unaware of CyberCindy's dilemma. CyberCindy finds her unfamiliar voice refreshing.

'God had to reveal himself on earth as either female or male – assuming of course that he was going to come in human form. So there was a fifty per cent chance it would be one or the other. Well, no, actually, that's probably not true.' She added quickly, contradicting herself. 'Jesus had to come as a man, or no one would have listened to him, such is the minority status of women. But Jesus' divinity is not entwined with his maleness, but with his humanness. Focussing on gender just causes division.'

'Too right!', CyberCindy interjected, thinking how different the Samaritan woman was to Ruth.

The woman appeared not to hear her and continued purposefully, 'If I thought that Jesus came to earth as a man, as opposed to a human, then speaking as a woman, I might just as well stop living. Don't you agree, CyberCindy?'

She stopped talking and looked to CyberCindy for affirmation. CyberCindy was taken aback at the woman's assumed inclusion of her spiritual sympathies. Ruth had always been on the defensive, or the attack. This woman was neither, and CyberCindy sensed she was sharing her doubts as much as her beliefs.

CyberCindy was about to reply along the lines that her life was valuable to her with or without Jesus, when the woman pre-empted her contribution and continued, 'Thinking along the same lines, Jesus came to earth as a Jew and not as a Samaritan. Does that mean then that in order to be like Jesus we have to be Jewish as well as male? I don't think so, though some may disagree, of course. Whilst our gender is God-given, and is utterly bound up in the people that we are, we can only really find our ultimate identity in God, not in our gender or race or class, and certainly not in the things we buy. It makes a mockery of life itself to try to forge an identity, when actually all we need do is take hold of the one that God has given us.'

Untidy clouds shift lazily across the sky. It doesn't seem as hot as it was previously. CyberCindy looks towards Mount Gerizim. She finds the woman's arguments attractive, although inwardly she reflects on the difficulty of taking hold of a God-given identity. Even if she were to believe this possible, how would she, in practical, everyday terms, take hold of such a thing?

There is a comfortable silence between the women, and CyberCindy is content to sit still for a moment and simply enjoy her surroundings. Gradually, she becomes conscious of an odd internal warmth flooding her body. She is unable to analyse this or assess it, and consciously considers the possibility that her Rompacomp may be overheating, or that some force may be trying to implant itself into her body. She checks the lights on her belt and all of them are functioning, as they should. She turns a knob and lifts up her visor on her SceneSensa, for she just wants to check her hardware. Nothing is burning; there is only a gentle hum and the usual green light indicating that she is travelling in cyberspace. She returns to the Samaritan woman, wondering whether she may be having some sort of spiritual experience. The warmth stays with her, mostly in her torso, although her fingers, too, feel hot and fluid. CyberCindy looks at the Samaritan woman and wonders if she has fallen in love with her, even if she is an avatar. The woman matches her gaze without embarrassment. They smile at each other.

'What is truth?', CyberCindy asks.

The Samaritan woman nods, acknowledging the question appreciatively. Her eyes gleam, almost mischievously, as she replies, 'Jesus is truth.'

The words hang in the air. CyberCindy was unprepared for the statement, and was expecting the woman to argue dogmatically for her own belief system. She did not expect the answer to be in terms of a person.

> ❝Now we see but a poor reflection as in a mirror; then we shall see face to face. Now I know in part, then I shall know fully, even as I am fully known (1 Corinthians 13:12).

> ❓ *It is not always necessary to claim objective certainty for the Christian life, even if there are objective realities which from a doctrinal perspective are crucial to faith. The Christian lives a life of faith. Christianity is full of paradox; to*

continually assert objective truth for every facet of life may sometimes, justifiably, be likened to an ostrich sticking its head in the sand. Whilst it is possible to know absolutely from a faith perspective, claims to absolutely know from a dogmatic perspective are arrogant, and not always helpful. There is much that is mysterious about God; and as little people, with little minds and hearts, we cannot possibly expect to embrace everything there is to know about God in our lifetime. That is why being a Christian is such an adventure. God's desire is that his people are in relationship with Him, and not excluded by their sin. Which is why Jesus went to the cross.

Whilst it is possible to know facts about God, which are unchangeable, an individual's relationship with God may deepen or perish irrespective of the facts. Christianity concerns relationship with a personal God, revealed by Jesus Christ, mediated by the Holy Spirit.

CyberCindy scoffs, 'Well why can't I meet him in virtual reality then?' She is almost angry.

Jesus in not a figure in a book; he is a living presence.[124]

Unperturbed by CyberCindy's aggression, the Samaritan woman replies, 'Perhaps you can, but not in the way you are expecting. You must remember, CyberCindy, that as a woman who was full of nationalistic pride, I was quite sure that my truth was the best truth. Having met Jesus, I am sure that his truth is the only truth. So I will try and share with you what I believe truth to be, but I have to confess to you that my understanding is marred by my own preconceptions and presuppositions.'

'Ooooh! Praise the Lord!', CyberCindy exclaims, half sincere, half teasing. 'And very postmodern,' she observes dryly, 'but please get on with it.' She is impatient.

The woman leans against the well, and cocks her head to one side, her hands gently locked together, her thumbs circling around one another once more.

'Jesus is the truth. He is God's truth, and he, being fully human and fully divine, is our perfect model for humanity. But there is always a danger that we might want to mould Jesus into our own image. I certainly did! When I thought of the Messiah, I thought of someone on my side, someone who would release us – the Samaritans – from oppression and serve my interests. It never occurred to me that I might need to change.'

orange

The woman stopped, and turned towards CyberCindy earnestly.

'But your question is good. My thinking is, that for too many of us, when we seek to discover truth, what we really want to do is justify our own cause, our own reason for living. In too many cases, it seems to me, believers have unintentionally promoted things which to God are anathema.'

'What sort of things?'

'Oh, things like apartheid, racism, sexism, injustice.'

'Why do you say that? It's me who's supposed to say those sorts of things! You're not allowed to be radical – you have to conform!'

'Conform? Conform to what? CyberCindy, knowing God is about as radical a relationship as I can ever expect to experience and I am deadly sincere in the things that I say.' The eyes narrow slightly, the big lips purse, the gentle face becomes taut and serious. 'But it seems to me, (probably because of the experience in my own life), that most people are unaware of their own blind spots, so when they come to read the Scriptures, they don't come to them fresh and alive to what the Spirit may be saying, but they come wanting God to rubber stamp their own ideology, which they perceive to be a good one.'

'Well,' CyberCindy says surprising even herself, 'that seems to me to be a rather cynical attitude, if you don't mind me saying so and not quite worthy of someone of your ilk.'

'My what?'

'Your ilk; your standing.'

'My standing? What standing is that?'

'Well, aren't you the one who Jesus uses to convert the Samaritans? Aren't you the first real evangelist in John's Gospel?'

'I've never considered that,' the woman replied,

'Well, you are, and in contrast to the learned religious leader and Pharisee Nicodemus, it is you that Jesus uses to spread the gospel, and it is to you that Jesus offers eternal life.'

'So that gives me a certain standing, does it?', the woman questions, secretly delighted that CyberCindy is arguing from knowledge rather than ignorance.

'Yes,' CyberCindy answers, 'Of course.' She is slightly confused at the Samaritan woman's odd perception of life.

'Hmm, well I don't really think you can single me out as being particularly special. Jesus called the disciples before he called me. And,' she pauses, smiling coquettishly, 'his offer of salvation is to everyone. God is working his purposes out in the course of history – his (God's) Story.'

'Corny cliché,' CyberCindy mutters.

The woman nods, 'Yes, I know, but a valuable cliché all the same. But, you know, Jesus is the Word become flesh. Words have power, because they are the means of communication. And God wants to communicate with his people. That is why he gave us Jesus, and that is why he gave us the Bible. John 1:1–5 says, "In the beginning was the Word and the Word was with God and the Word was God. He was with God in the beginning. Through him all things were made, without him nothing was made that has been made. In him was life and that life was the light of all people. The light shines in the darkness, but the darkness has not understood it."'

'But how can we know what is the light?', CyberCindy asked, her frustration increasing, 'And why do you insist on calling God HE all the time?!'

Our little systems have their day;
They have their day and cease to be:
They are but broken lights of thee,
And thou, O Lord, art more than they.[125]

'CyberCindy, we have to believe that words can correspond to reality, that mutual understanding is the norm. But in the English language we have male and female pronouns. Jesus came as a man and taught his disciples to call God father. That is not because he wants the world to understand that male is best. It is because he wants the world to understand that he is a personal God.'

'So could you call God HER then?'

'Well, some believers can, I can't. Jesus is too personal to me. You see, Jesus is divine and he is male, so I do call God 'He'. But let's not get sidetracked. John's Gospel calls Jesus the Word. God's whole agenda is communication. He just wants relationship with his people. That's what life is all about.'

'

Today, life is a choice of insanities.
Success, failure, love, chastity, debauchery,
money or soviets
It is a string of insanities.
All insane.
Why not stay out, and learn to contain oneself?[126]

blue

'But,' CyberCindy interrupts, 'it isn't possible to know what the Word means is it? It isn't possible to know was going on in some parts of the Bible, is it? I mean, why did Ruth go and uncover Boaz's feet (if it was his feet she uncovered)? What significance is there in that? No one knows, do they! You can't claim to know everything, can you?', she exclaims, triumphantly.

'Well, maybe, not. But perhaps CyberCindy, you are asking the wrong questions. Maybe it doesn't matter – significantly – that Ruth uncovered Boaz's feet. The point is, she went to him. She asked. She was the activist. We can't hope to know the whole historical, cultural, social, political or religious background. But we can look at her and what she did in the context of the Bible and of our knowledge of those times.'

'The Bible, the Bible, that's all you guys ever say to me. But it's so boring!', CyberCindy was exasperated.

'Why do you say it's boring, when you keep wanting to talk with Ruth and me?', the Samaritan woman asked.

There is a pause whilst CyberCindy considers her answer, 'Well, l get an instant reaction from you. Communication is easy. When I read the Bible, I have to think about it. I'm just not used to that!'

'Interesting,' the Samaritan woman says gently, 'I suppose that, if you read it on your own, it will be boring. You need the Holy Spirit to lead and guide you.'

'The Holy Spirit?', CyberCindy was surprised, 'What's the Holy Spirit? I thought you Christians weren't into things spiritual.'

'What do you mean?', the Samaritan woman asked, unable to conceal her surprise.

'Well, I thought being a Christian is all about doing what God wants. You know, living out what you think is a morally righteous sort of life. Good and evil and all that. That's not very spiritual is it?'

The Samaritan woman, though she smiled, was confused. 'You mean, you don't think there is a spiritual dimension to the Christian life?', she asks.

'Well is there?', CyberCindy asks, amazed that the woman seems to think differently.

'What do you think Jesus is offering me when he talks about living water?', the Samaritan woman asks.

'Wet stuff.'

CyberCindy smirks, knowing that she will irritate the woman, but the woman ignores her response and continues, 'Jesus is the source of all life. He gives us physical, material life. And then he gives us spiritual, eternal life, which leads to full communion with God.'

> 'Any view that restricts the Spirit to authenticating and enforcing what is written in Scripture is quite inadequate in the light of Jesus' own promises about the creative action of the Spirit in the Church.'[127]

> 'Nothing the Spirit says or does can ever contradict what Jesus said and did.'[128]

> 'The Spirit will expose, explicate, interpret and apply the truth as it is in Christ in a way that is faithful to its first biblical exposition but that goes far beyond it and relates the same truth to questions and situations that are quite different from any Jesus or the apostles encountered and dealt with.'[129]

The Samaritan looks around her at the scenery, relishing the moment, unaware that CyberCindy is distancing herself mentally from her argument. She continues, 'Looking back, I think it is hilarious that I refuse him a drink, thinking that my water is better than his water. Oh, CyberCindy, I was so full of myself, and my tradition, and my historical and theological knowledge, I nearly missed out on eternal life!'

Then to CyberCindy's surprise and embarrassment, the woman lifts her head to the sky and laughs, and leaps up, spreading her dark skirt about her, running for joy around the well, giving a loud 'Whoop!' as she does so. She giggles spontaneously, knowing her behaviour to be ridiculous, lifting her knees high in a strange dance, finishing with an energetic twirl, landing with a heavy thud beside CyberCindy, breathing heavily before taking up her story.

'Let me explain. Samaria, as you surely know by now, is a land of spiritual darkness, for it has compromised its Jewish roots. But as providence would have it (you would say chance, I expect), Jesus – the wonderful Jewish rabbi – finds himself resting by Jacob's well in the bright light of day, and lo and behold, a woman (that is, me), comes to draw water. You see, I am a perfect example of what John 1:12–13 claims: I am not born of natural descent (as Jews are), because I am a

183

Samaritan. I am not born of human decision, because there is no way I would have chosen to follow Christ without God's intervention. And I am not born of a husband's will for I have no husband. I have been born of God, born first into this life and born second into eternal life. Let me show you what I mean.'

green

The woman darts to a nearby bush and returns with a
handful of wool, which she moulds purposefully into a
definite shape, poking her finger through to make a hole at
one end. Then she raises the wool to her face,
transforming it into a makeshift beard, placing the hole
over her mouth, and she says, 'Give me a drink' in a deep
voice. Then taking away the beard, she stands straight,
looking directly ahead, taking the part of narrator, 'says
Source of All Life'. Turning right round, she impersonates
herself and responds aggressively, 'Oooh! Not on your
nelly! I'm not sharing my bucket with the likes of you!'

CyberCindy laughs.

The woman returns the beard to her mouth, 'If you knew
who I was you would ask me for a drink'.

'Oh really? Well, even if I asked you, you couldn't give me
a drink – you haven't got a bucket ... anyway any water
that you, a Jew could give me, wouldn't be half as good as
the water from this well. This water belonged to my father
Jacob and watered himself, his sons and his animals, and
continues to water me, thank you very much.'

She sticks her tongue out at the imaginary Jesus and skips
joyfully around the well, delighting in the ridiculousness
of her show. CyberCindy is captivated by this
extraordinary and unexpected drama. Then, beard to
mouth, and deep tones, 'The water I give is far superior
to this water, because it quenches thirst forever,' beard
down, looking straight ahead, 'says Source of All Life'.

185

'Well, if it does that, then sonny, you better give me some,' in mocking tone.

Beard to mouth, stern voice, 'Not unless your husband says you can have it.'

A pause. A look. A near-stammer. 'I haven't got a husband,' she says almost, trying to say it victoriously, but the words make naked the woman's vulnerability. Then beard to mouth, 'Too right you haven't, you've had five, and what's more you're not married to the chap you're living with now.'

'Ooooh! Very clever, I must say! I see you're a Prophet with a capital P. Well if you're so clever, tell me this then,' the woman turns aside to CyberCindy, pointing her finger towards where the imaginary Jesus is standing, and says, pantomime fashion, 'Smarty-pants'.

CyberCindy chuckles. The woman really is very funny.

She faces the imaginary Jesus once more and says with all seriousness, a trace of vindictiveness underlying her question, 'Why don't you Jews worship here, on this mountain that our fathers worshipped on, eh? 'Cos we Samaritans are better than you Jews.'

The woman spits on the ground and lifts her head to the air, holding her skirt with magisterial pomp. Then she picks up the beard, which had fallen from her grasp as she had enthusiastically spat, and returns it to her chin. A deep voice replies to her provocation, 'I don't think so, for salvation comes from the Jews. Besides, the time is coming when it won't matter where you worship, it'll matter how you worship.'

The woman exaggerates her response to Jesus and looks aghast. She gathers herself together, and asserts herself once more, 'Well, I don't know about that,' she says 'but

I do know,' (aside to CyberCindy) 'because I know about these things and he doesn't,' (returning again to the imaginary Jesus,) 'someone who will, and that's the Messiah!'

She says this with great triumph, raising herself to her full height, her chest heaving dramatically. There is a pause, before the woman slowly brings the beard to her chin once more and says, penetratingly, 'Oh yes? Well, I am he'.

She stands absolutely still before lifting her arms to the air and presenting herself to an imaginary but appreciative audience, finishing with a low bow. CyberCindy claps spontaneously, shouting, 'Bravo! Bravo!', unaware that at that moment she is applauding a fictitious character inhabiting a fictitious world.

The woman beams; she is pleased with her performance.

> ❜ John employs the archetypal modes of storytelling in general, as described from a literary-critical perspective by Frye: comedy, romance, satire/irony and tragedy.[130]

'CyberCindy, Jesus is the one with whom there is eternal life, he is the one who gives spiritual satisfaction, and he is the one who is justifiably intolerant of human intolerance, for He is divine. Jesus is God's perfect revelation of himself.'

As the woman is speaking, CyberCindy notices a small crowd coming towards them from the village. There is an air of excitement and expectancy about them as they gravitate animatedly towards the two women.

CyberCindy's enjoyment of the past few moments is immediately disturbed. She is fearful of their approach, and for some reason which she fails to determine, she feels threatened by them. As the crowd reaches the well, the people turn directly to CyberCindy in unison and say, 'We no longer believe just because of what she said; now we have heard for ourselves and we know that Jesus really is the Saviour of the world.'[131]

Then, before she has time to respond, the scene jumps, as if an earthquake, and she hears the Samaritan woman repeat, 'Jesus is God's perfect revelation of himself', and witnesses the crowd approaching the well once more, who turn again and simultaneously repeat,

'We no longer believe just because of what she said; now we have heard for ourselves and we know that Jesus really is the Saviour of the world.'

CyberCindy wants to get away from this unexpected and uncalled for onslaught. She feels as if she is in a nightmare. Her mind feels constrained and tight; her breathing quickens, and her heart pumps the blood rapidly around her body. The warm feeling is still within her, but it brings no comfort. She suspects that she is going to faint. Why is the crowd speaking to her in this way? Who asked them to intervene, to come and impress their own agenda on her? What right do they have to interrupt her conversation, to intrude on her happiness? There is another earthquake, and the Samaritan woman once again turns to her to repeat her last sentence, but CyberCindy does not give her time to begin. She realises that there is a technical fault in this virtual world, and exits rapidly, pleased to escape but disappointed by the persecution of the villagers. Angry and aggrieved, CyberCindy exits the amateur virtual world of Sychar. Once home, she has a shower, after which she lies on her bed, and leafs through the Bible, sometimes reading one or two verses, sometimes a whole passage, wondering if it is true.

The Samaritan woman flips across cyber worlds towards Ruth, who she finds waiting for her. Ruth is standing by the front door of her home, goats and chickens meandering nearby, Obed asleep in the arms of Naomi, who is sitting just inside the door.

'Well?', Ruth asks, a sense of urgency in her tone.

'I don't know,' says the Samaritan woman with a sense of exasperation, 'I think we need to pray.'

red, orange, yellow, green, blue, indigo, violet

CyberCindy takes Australian Michael to the art gallery
and shows him the painting of the old lady in the storm.
She notices, to her surprise, that it is for sale. Australian
Michael likes the picture, and explains that the patch of
blue is a symbol to him of hope, that the future is not as
bleak as it might appear. CyberCindy smiles wryly. He
buys the picture and gives it to her as a thank you for her
generosity to him. Later, alone in her apartment, she
hangs the picture on the wall, placing it so that she can
see it whilst sitting beside Toby. She sits down and gazes
at the picture.

CyberCindy cannot take her eyes off the little patch of
blue sky.

Appendix 1

'The Samaritan Woman's Story': A Modern Approach
(of little interest to CyberCindy)
Background Information on John 4:1–42

Introduction

John's Gospel was written so 'that you may believe' (John 20:30–31), with a two-fold purpose: to create faith and encourage discipleship. The Gospel weaves theology, history, and narrative together in a multi-stranded chord so that intellectual faith is always challenged to radical discipleship. It was probably written about 80–90 AD, after the fall of Jerusalem, most likely by John, son of Zebedee, one of Jesus' closest disciples. Bauckham puts forward an interesting argument that the author, the 'beloved disciple,' could have been Lazarus.[132]

For the purposes of analysing John 4:1–42, we may split the passage into six, each passage following on from the proceeding one and leading logically on to the next, thus:

4:1–3   The persecuted Jesus leaves Judea.
4:4–6   The setting.

4:7–26 Theological dialogue between Jesus and the woman of Samaria.

4:27–33 Theological questions asked by the disciples, woman and townsfolk.

4:34–38 Theological answers – Jesus' mission/disciples mission.

4:39–42 Happy ending.

4:1–3: *The Persecuted Jesus Leaves Judea*

Biblical background

Following Jesus' attack on the Jerusalem Temple at Passover, a Pharisee named Nicodemus comes to Jesus, not in secret as has often been assumed, but on behalf of the Jewish ruling council (v. 1), for he says, 'Rabbi, we know' (v. 2) and seeks theological discussion with this man from God, essentially on the necessity of baptism (John 3:3–7), discussing it as a religious leader responsible for those who would seek to live by the truth (v. 21). Significantly, he visits Jesus at night (John 3:1), for men love darkness (John 3:19).

John 3:25 tells us that 'an argument developed between some of John's disciples and a certain Jew over the matter of ceremonial washing'. This certain Jew was undoubtedly Nicodemus, who following his conversation with Jesus has gone to John's disciples with more questions and queries, stirring up trouble for the one who advocates a second birth of water and the Spirit (John 3:5), and wanting to know if John's disciples are in sympathy with Jesus' mission. In answer to his disciples' concerns, John the Baptist identifies Jesus as the Christ, the bridegroom, (John 3:27–30) and before we come to chapter 4, John states 'Whoever believes in the Son has eternal life, but whoever rejects the Son will not see life, for God's wrath remains on him' (v. 36).

Verses 4:1–3 testify to Jesus' persecution by the Pharisees, (for whom Nicodemus was the catalyst), to his growing popularity, and sensitivity to his cousin John's ministry.

John 4:4–6: The Setting

The start of the story

Jesus, (the Word become flesh (John 1:14)) reaches his forefather Jacob's well, weary and tired, at the height of the day and in the full heat and light of the sun. In this way, the writer sets the scene for the revelation to follow, for 'whoever lives by the truth comes into the light, so that it might be seen plainly that what he has done has been done through God' (John 3:21).

John 7–26: Theological Dialogue – Jesus and the Woman of Samaria

The comedy commences

Jesus, (in whom was life, the light of men, (John 1:1)) asks the Samaritan woman for a drink (v. 7).[133] In so doing, Jesus, the Jewish Rabbi engages with the nameless Samaritan female, God's holy and appointed one reaches out to a second class race and the second class sex, apparently disregarding cultural norms and expectations. The woman is not impressed, but affronted (v. 9), and the writer feels obliged to offer an explanation for her refusal to comply with the simple request.[134] Jesus takes umbrage (v. 10) and cannot help revealing through his enigmatic speech that he is superior to her, for although he just wants a drink of water (in his human-capacity) it is he who brings others to eternal life (in his God-capacity) (John 1:14).[135] Having just come hotfoot from a successful ministry baptising believers, it is gruelling for Jesus to suffer the rebuttal of someone claiming to have a sounder knowledge of culture and religion than he (v. 9).[136] The woman again questions Jesus' claim to superiority, firstly exposing it at face value as impractical nonsense (v. 11), and secondly recognising the claim of superiority that Jesus has made, and asking him if he is greater than Jacob (v. 12). In response to this Jesus affirms that he is not talking about practical physical water, but spiritual water which leads to eternal life (vv. 13–14). The woman appears to like this idea for she submits to Jesus' sales talk (v. 15), and asks for some of this special water, so that she need not come to gather water any more at the well. The woman calls Jesus' bluff, but he turns the tables on the woman, for he tells her to go and get her husband (v. 16).[137]

In the first century women were still largely the property of men, so in order for this conversation to really lead to eternal life, Jesus wants the woman's husband to be present.[138] Present for what? To witness her conversion? Is Jesus still thinking along the lines of baptism? Very possibly. However, he has exposed the woman's area of weakness, for she has to confess that she has no husband, and Jesus takes his cue to expose the fact that he really is superior to her, and to their forefather Jacob, for he knows all her history (vv. 17–18). The woman concedes Jesus' prophetic insight and continues talking in a theological vein, emphasising again cultural and theological differences which have for centuries meant that Jews and Samaritans are divided from one another, despite a common heritage ('our fathers worshipped on this mountain, but you Jews claim'; v. 20).[139] Jesus is forced into the defensive once more, and hits a punch aimed to scatter and shatter the woman's perspective (vv. 21–24). He tells her the time is coming when these differences will be irrelevant, that salvation is from the Jews, and that 'God's worshippers must worship in spirit and truth' (v. 24). The woman, who has finally had the rug taken from under her feet, now wishes to draw the conversation to a close, and concludes that neither Jesus nor she can know everything, but when the Messiah comes, he will explain all (v. 25). Jesus now plays his trump card, the card that will overturn the woman's life: 'I who speak to you am he.' he says (v. 26).[140]

It is often argued or assumed that the Samaritan woman is a person of loose morals, who, because of her low standing in the community, comes to the well alone, at the height of the noonday sun, because of her shame and exclusion from society.[141] However, when Rebekkah in Genesis 24:17ff. does the same, it is not regarded as odd that she goes to the well apparently alone. The most telling evidence against this woman is that the man with whom she is now living is not her husband (v. 18), and although she has had five husbands, we are not told why.[142] Women did not have rights then as they do today, and wives could not divorce husbands. Her situation could have resulted from a lack of responsibility on the part of her successive husbands, who may have regarded her simply as a commodity whom they could dispose of when she displeased them in any way.[143] Or she may have outlived her husbands, whose brothers may have married her in obedience to Levirate law. Maybe a mixture of both, we do not know, but five marriages and one live-in boyfriend don't necessarily make this woman a prostitute, they may simply make her a (dependent) commodity for men to pick up and drop as they fancy. No wonder she takes issue with Jesus (v. 9).

From the manner with which she talks to Jesus, which is one of cantankerous well-ingrained nationalistic pride, and from her history of having had five husbands, and from her desire to be relieved of this onerous task of water collecting, we may surmise that the woman is elderly, or at least no flighty young thing. She is steeped in her own culture and religious teaching, and going to the well for water she meets an apparently ignorant young Jewish rabbi. Far from being a simpleton, or a flirt, this Samaritan plays Jesus at his own game and questions theological truth from her own perspective and identity as a Samaritan.[144]

John 4:27–30: Theological Questions – Disciples, Woman and Townsfolk

What is he doing and who does he think he is?

The disciples return, surprised that Jesus is talking to a woman. Was this because they had left him tired and resting, with little energy for dialogue; was it because Jesus was talking to a woman; or was it because Jesus, a man, was talking to a woman, or was it because Jesus the Jew was talking to a Samaritan? Who knows?[145]

The woman, excited by the possibility that the man with whom she has been talking could be the one for whom she has been waiting (John 3:21), leaving her mission to the well to fetch water unfinished ('leaving her water jar'; v. 28), returns to the town and implores the folk to come and see the 'man who told me everything I ever did', asking, 'Could this be the Christ?' (v. 29).[146] The townsfolk act upon her witness and make their way to see Jesus for themselves. One wonders if the woman, with such a sound grasp of her own identity and theology, is a prophetess, for she is clearly looking forward to the day when the Messiah comes (v. 25), she clearly has a theological agenda (vv. 9, 12, 19, 20) and she is clearly in good standing within her community (vv. 30, 39, 40).

John 4:31–38: Theological Answers – Jesus' Mission/Disciples Mission

The moral of the story

Jesus' disciples, who paid little attention to his need for water and followed their own agenda by going into the (Samaritan) town to buy food (v. 8), urge Jesus to reward their efforts by eating something (v. 31). Jesus again asserts his superiority over the disciples 'I have food to eat that you know nothing about' (v. 32) and the disciples are left wondering (perhaps) if the woman has provided a picnic for Jesus (v. 33).

Jesus then begins to teach his disciples that his sustenance comes from doing 'the will of him who sent me and to finish his work' (v. 34). Emulating the Samaritan woman, who appeared to surmise that Jesus' water would satisfy all her physical needs (v. 15), Jesus now tells his disciples that his food, to do the will of the one who sent him, negates the need for physical food. Not only is Jesus fed in this way – there is plenty of food to eat, for the fields are ripe for harvest (v. 35) – but this is food that the disciples appear not to know anything about, for Jesus tells them, 'Even now the reaper draws his wages, even now, he harvests the crop for eternal life' (v. 36). Drawing on his knowledge of what the Samaritan woman is currently doing – witnessing to his arrival and drawing others to investigate his claims for themselves – Jesus is preparing his disciples to receive these new converts, whom, (speculatively), they may baptise (John 4:2), even though they have played no role in the conversion (v. 38).[147]

John 4:39–42: Happy Ending

We know who he is

Through the woman's testimony, many of the Samaritans believe in Jesus (v. 39); they urge him to stay and many more become believers 'because of his words' (vv. 40–41) The Samaritan townsfolk confirm to the woman that their faith is not based solely on her witness, rather it is based on having met Jesus themselves, and now they can proclaim that this Jesus, 'really is the Saviour of the world', in other words, that he is the much-longed for Christ (v. 42 cf. v. 29b).

If one takes into account the form-critical betrothal-type scene, and John's description of Jesus as the bridegroom (John 3:29), we may agree with some narrative interpretations which claim this account is preparing us to expect that Jesus and the Samaritan woman are pursuing the possibility of marriage.[148] Despite the fact that no marriage occurs, there is also the possibility of a (wedding) feast (John 4:34–38). It would seem then, that marriage is on the agenda. But there is no obvious wedding. Yet ... whilst there is no marriage in terms of the individual relationship between Jesus and the woman, through Jesus' ministry, as Saviour of the world, the nationalistic hatred between Jew and Samaritan is thwarted. Jew and Samaritan are at last wedded together as the Saviour of the world, the fulfilment of eschatological hope (John 4:26) brings unity where there was division. He is the fulfilment of the entire Samaritans' hopes; he is their expected Messiah. In his interchange with the woman, and with his disciples, Jesus crosses boundaries of culture, tradition, theology, gender and nationalism. This account therefore is not merely a historical one of a discussion Jesus has with a woman at a well. It has profound theological significance as the nature of Jesus' role and ministry is revealed: that the Word, who became flesh, and who takes away the sin of the world, is the saviour of the world. Division is no longer an authentic position to hold.

Notes

1 G. Bailey, *Stuff and Nonsense: A Collection of Verse and Worse*, 11.
2 D. Lyon, *Postmodernity*, 12.
3 See G.E. Veith, *Guide to Contemporary Culture*, for more detailed argument.
4 Augustine, *Confessions*.
5 R. Radford Ruether, *Sexism and God-Talk: Toward a Feminist Theology*, 23.
6 Dip into the *IVP Women's Bible Commentary* (eds Kroeger and Evans) written 'by women of faith who believe that all Scripture is inspired by God and given for the benefit of all humanity', for fascinating insights into the Scriptures, xiv.
7 D. Tomlinson, *The Post-Evangelical*, 37.
8 Not recommended ... but it's your decision.
9 Highly recommended.
10 If you choose F3 please understand that this is an interpretation and is in no way intended to replace the biblical account, but to provide the background with which to proceed as you read the rest of this book.
11 Judges were legal advisers as well as leaders, and people of action, who delivered the Israelites from subjection to the nations around them and became rulers, raised up by God to govern the people, politically and religiously.
12 Deuteronomy 23:3–6.
13 Genesis 18:30–38.
14 Numbers 25:1–5.
15 In those distant days, a family belonged to a clan (an extended family), and the clan belonged to a tribe. There were twelve tribes of

Israel, and each one had descended from the twelve sons of Jacob. After the Israelites entered Canaan, and after some fierce fighting, the land was shared out amongst the tribes. The Old Testament books of Joshua and Judges give detailed historical information. A family would have a clear identity. It would share festivals and celebrations with clan members, and members of one tribe inhabited whole towns and cities. Loyalty to the tribe was absolute; you were born into it, you married within it, you died a member of it. It was in this way that the Israelites, God's chosen people, protected themselves against the vagaries of the other peoples living around them. They would avenge blood for blood if a clan member was maimed or killed they would 'own' one another's calamities and victories; to dishonour a member of one's family, clan or tribe, was a serious offence and individuals within these groups would personally take it upon themselves to maintain justice, law and order, by seeking retribution. Similarly, one's esteem would be greatly enhanced if one's tribe, clan or family had won prestigious acclaim in some way.

16 In those long-ago days, women were reliant on men for their welfare. A father would protect and provide for his daughter. A husband would do likewise for his wife. Sons would care for their widowed mother. If a woman had no father, no husband and no sons, she had no protection and no provision. In short, she became a nobody, with no voice and no value. Her only hope was that male members of the clan would care for her, in honour of her men folk.

17 Their journey could have been anything from about forty to over one hundred miles.

18 Ruth leaves her native Moab to settle in Judah, just as Jesus Christ some years later left the realms of heaven to identify with and redeem the world.

19 The gleaning laws of that day protected both the poor and the foreign living amongst Israelite society, categories which Ruth well satisfied (Leviticus 19:9–10 and 23:22). God was not reinforcing a patriarchal cultural framework through the laws which allowed gleaning, but simply securing a little dignity for the vulnerable and needy, something which in principle we would like to agree with, but in practice like to overlook. The poor and the foreign, whilst not under condemnation from more respectable elements of Israelite society, would be obliged to suffer what came with their lowly status: disregard and disrespect. Harvesters no doubt despised

gleaners, for not only did they fall within the lowest stratum of society, a gleaner on the land meant less of a harvest. So if gleaners could be 'encouraged' to work in someone else's field, so much the better. Fields were not marked out by boundaries, but rather by knowledge that the field on the left belonged to so-and-so, and the field on the right belonged to that-so-and-so. Ownership was passed down from one family to another; through the generations.

20 Ruth, the wife of Mahlon and daughter-in-law of Elimelech, even though a Moabite, would clearly have greater standing than Boaz's servant girls had circumstances treated her more kindly. She is not slow to share her humiliation with Boaz, a man of obvious good reputation.

21 Boaz has done good to the living by allowing Ruth to glean; he has done good to the dead by honouring Elimelech and Mahlon in being good to Ruth.

22 Family (kinsman) redeemers were those males closest in line to surviving females. Their role within the clan was to ensure that the honour and integrity of their deceased relative was maintained. This could be done in a number of ways. If the survivors of a family were so destitute that it was necessary to sell the family land, it was the role of the kinsman redeemer to 'buy back' the land (i.e. redeem it) and keep it in the clan. The kinsman redeemer may also have been expected to play the separate role of *levir*. If a man died leaving no male heir, his closest male relative was required to marry his widow. The first-born son of this union would be regarded as the dead man's child, thus maintaining the family line and name. However, if there were no second son in this union, the *levir* would have sacrificed his own family line for the sake of the dead man's. Accordingly, the practice of levirate marriage was not always upheld, as in the case of Tamar and Judah (Genesis 38). Women could not enforce it, being the vulnerable party. They relied solely on the honour and dignity which family members applied to their clan. To have a man to whom you were answerable gave you a status. A man represented, according to his reputation, security, protection, affiliation.

23 It is ironic that Naomi plays the part of seeking to ensure Ruth's security, when initially it was Ruth who was seeking to secure Naomi's.

24 In Hebrew, feet (*regel*) (vv. 4, 7, 8) is sometimes used as an euphemism for the sexual organs. The text is therefore ambiguous

for modern readers. All we can conclude is that the issue of a sexual encounter here is not an important part of the story. Some interpretations are emphatic in claiming there was no sexual intercourse; whilst this can be argued, it is unnecessary to do so. There are many instances of immorality in the Old Testament. The people whom God chooses to work his purposes out are usually flawed (e.g. Abraham was a liar, Genesis 12:12–13; Moses was a murderer, Exodus 2:12; David was an adulterer, 2 Samuel 11). If a man had intercourse with a woman, he was obliged to marry her. So, given that there was a closer kinsman-redeemer who had a right to redeem Naomi's land, it would not have served Ruth or Boaz's interests if others had known she had visited him at night on the threshing floor (Ruth 3:14). But the text is inconclusive and all we can be sure of is that Ruth is claiming Boaz as her *goel*, her kinsman redeemer, and thus is once again fully identifying herself with her Israelite husband, his people and his God. She may be proposing marriage; but *levir* is not mentioned here. It transpires later, in Chapter 4, that Ruth has sought Boaz's help in redeeming some land that Naomi had to sell. Perhaps Naomi is offering this land as a form of dowry, should Boaz be willing to marry Ruth.

25 Ruth, the one who sought to protect Naomi, and for whom Boaz sought to confer Yahweh's protection, is appealing to Boaz to fulfil this by asking him to give her protection.

26 The Man With No Name is not prepared to risk his own family line for the sake of Mahlon's or even Elimelech's. Buying the land, and acting as *goel* is one thing. Acting as *levir* and securing a child on behalf of Mahlon or on behalf of Elimelech is quite another. Ruth and The Man with No Name would need to have two boys in order for him to keep his name with his own estate. The elder one would secure Mahlon's line, and the younger would be regarded as The Man with No Name's firstborn and inherit his estate. If there was no second boy, the older son would inherit everything, and this would mean that the Man with No Name had forfeited his line for Mahlon's. So far Ruth does not have a good track record in the baby begetting stakes.

27 Ironically, Elimelech's name does not feature in Ruth's genealogy.

28 Rachel and Leah were Jacob's wives and the mothers of twelve sons, the sons from whom the twelve tribes of Israel were named.

29 This is perhaps a self-fulfilling prophecy, in that if Ruth had a son by Boaz then he would inevitably be of the line of Perez, as would a son

had he been born to Mahlon, as they are in the same clan. Judah was one of the twelve sons of Jacob; his son Perez is the patriarch of the family line recorded at the end of Ruth, culminating with David, the great King. It is through this family line comes that Jesus, the Messiah, is born.

30 'Images by Murden Woods', in J. Grana, (ed), *Images: Women in Transition*, 15.

31 M. Benedikt, *Cyberspace: First Steps*, 122.

32 Ibid.

33 D. Atkinson, *The Message of Ruth*, 3.

34 Ruether, *Sexism*, 179.

35 Ibid., 179.

36 E. Campbell Jr, *Ruth*, 29.

37 R.M. Hals, *Theology of Ruth*, 75.

38 See the Bibliography for evidence of this, if you want to.

39 Rashkow, 'Ruth: The Discourse of Power and the Power of Discourse', in A. Brenner (ed.), *A Feminist Companion to Ruth*, 26.

40 D. Harvey, *The Condition of Postmodernity*, 45.

41 Ibid., 65.

42 *boING boING* is a typically 'postmodern' magazine: colloquially termed a zine.

43 Judges 21:25.

44 E. Kübler-Ross, *On Death and Dying*.

45 Deuteronomy 23:4.

46 Meike Bal, 'Heroism and Proper Names, or the Fruits of Analogy', in A. Brenner, (ed), *A Feminist Companion to Ruth*, 42–69; also L.L. Bronner, 'A Thematic Approach to Ruth in Rabbinic Literature', in A. Brenner, (ed), *A Feminist Companion to Ruth*, 146–69, esp. 153.

47 Harvey, *Condition*, 345.

48 Luke 1:35.

49 K. Tester, 'Postmodernism', *Sociology* 11.7 (1995), 133.

50 See P. Sampson, 'The Rise of Postmodernity', in Sampson, P., V. Samuel & C. Sugden (eds.), *Faith and Modernity*, 34.

51 Bailey, *Stuff and Nonsense*, 66.

52 Atkinson, *Message*, 16.

53 Stevie Smith, *Selected Poems*, 40.

54 A. Borrowdale, *A Woman's Work: Changing Christian Attitudes*, 83.

55 W. Somerset Maugham, 'The Circle', cited in Borrowdale, *Woman's Work*.

56 Ruether, *Sexism*, 188.
57 S. Thistlethwaite, *Sex, Race & God*, 78.
58 See E. Storkey, *What's Right with Feminism?*.
59 Borrowdale, *Woman's Work*, 32.
60 C. Ramazogonoglu, 'Gender', Sociology, 7.6 (1990), 139.
61 Ruether, *Sexism*, 74.
62 Thistlethwaite, *Sex*, 79.
63 'The Color Purple', cited in Thistlethwaite, *Sex*, 89.
64 de Tocqueville quoted in Lyon, *Postmodernity*, 33.
65 Lyon, *Postmodernity*, 33
66 Ramazanoglu, 'Gender', 143.
67 Ruether, *Sexism*, 35.
68 N. Mercer, 'Postmodernity and Rationality: The Final Credits or Just a Commercial Break?', in Antony Billington, Tony Lane & Max Turner (eds.), *Mission and Meaning: Essays Presented to Peter Cotterell*, 336.
69 Veith, *Contemporary Culture*, 198.
70 Mercer, 'Postmodernity and Rationality', 333.
71 Scraton & Bramham, 'Leisure and Postmodernity', 22 in *Sociology* 11 (1995).
72 Lyons, *Postmodernity*, 21.
73 E. Brunner quoted in R. Cook, 'Postmodernism, Pluralism and John Hick', *Themelios* 19.1 (Oct 1993), 12.
74 Sampson, 'Rise of Postmodernity', 30.
75 Highly recommended.
76 Robert Browning, 'The Ring and the Book', VI. 2038, in *The Complete Poetical Works of Robert Browning* Vol. 8, 156.
77 John 4:9.
78 John 4:10.
79 John 4:11.
80 John 4:13–14.
81 John 4:15.
82 John 4:16.
83 John 4:17a.
84 John 4:17, 18.
85 John 4:19–20.
86 John 4:21–24.
87 John 4:25.
88 John 4:26.
89 John 4:31.

90 John 4:32.

91 John 4:34–38.

92 Nehemiah 13, cf. Jos, Anti. xi 297–347, esp. 340; quoted in D.A. Carson, *The Gospel According to John*, 216. The Samaritans were 'soiled, tarnished and impure; politically untrustworthy and religiously heretical'.

93 Carson, *John*, 216.

94 G.A. Phillips, 'The Ethics of Reading Deconstructively, or Speaking Face-to-Face: The Samaritan Woman Meets Derrida at the Well', in E.S. Malbon and E.V. McKnight (eds.), *The New Literary Criticism and the New Testament*, 317.

95 R.A. Culpepper, *Anatomy of the Fourth Gospel: A Study in Literary Design*, 236.

96 M.W.G. Stibbe, *John's Gospel*, 32.

97 S.M. Schneiders, 'Women in the Fourth Gospel and the Role of Women in the Contemporary Church', *Biblical Theology Bulletin* 12.2 (April 1982), 36.

98 Collingwood, 235; cited in Stibbe, *John's Gospel*, 32.

99 G. O'Day, *Revelation in the Fourth Gospel: Narrative Mode and Theological Claim*, 90–2. There is a thin theological line to be drawn between God speaking through his 'inerrant Word' and through his Holy Spirit; for some exegetes, this line is not discernible.

100 John 15:26; 2 Timothy 3:16.

101 John 1:28, 39b, 43, 44; 3:22; 4:1–6; 54; 5:2, etc.

102 See A. Brenner, *The Israelite Woman: Social Role and Literary Type in Biblical Narrative*, 116.

103 C.H. Talbert, *Reading John: A Literary and Theological Commentary on the Fourth Gospel and the Johannine Epistles*, 112.

104 R.G. Maccini, *Her Testimony is True: Women as Witness according to John*, 135.

105 D.M. Patte, *Ethics of Biblical Interpretation: A Re-evaluation*, 101.

106 E. Schüssler Fiorenza, *Bread Not Stone, The Challenge of Biblical Interpretation*, 118.

107 Kroeger and Evans, (eds) *IVP Women's Bible*, xiv.

108 John 4:7, 10, 14.

109 John 4:26.

110 John 4:18.

111 John 4:14, 23.

112 Schüssler Fiorenza, *Bread*, 141.

113 J. Stott, *Issues Facing Christians Today*, 290.

114 Carson, *John*, 216.

115 Maccini, *Her Testimony*, 135.

116 See Talbert, *Reading John* and Maccini, *Her Testimony*; also Carson, *John*, 227.

117 Storkey, *What's Right with Feminism?*, 161.

118 Reprinted by kind permission of Phil Burt, Copyright 1986 Horrobin/Leavers Junior Praise, Marshall Pickering.

119 Exodus 3:14.

120 John 8:58.

121 Reprinted by kind permission of P. Bihorn. Copyright *Junior Praise*, Marshall Pickering.

122 John Milton, 'Paradise Lost', VIII. 488 in H.C. Beeching (ed.), *The Poetical Works of John Milton*.

123 Stibbe, *John's Gospel*, 67–8.

124 W. Barclay, *The Gospel of Matthew*, Vol. 1, 234.

125 Alfred, Lord Tennyson, 'In Memoriam A.H.H.', V, in *The Complete Works of Alfred Lord Tennyson*, 247.

126 D.H. Lawrence, 'Today' in Vivian de Sola Pinto and Warren Roberts, *The Complete Poems of D.H. Lawrence*, 839.

127 T.A. Smail, *The Giving Gift: The Holy Spirit in Person*, 75.

128 Ibid.

129 Ibid.

130 Stibbe, *John's Gospel*, 32–72.

131 John 4:42.

132 R. Bauckham, 'The Beloved Disciple as Ideal Author', *JSNT* 49 (1993), 21–44.

133 J. Fenton, *Finding the Way through John*, 22, suggests that it is remarkable that John chooses a woman to become both a believer and a witness, and not a Jewish woman, or indeed just any woman, but a Samaritan woman. He states that John could scarcely have made a more unexpected choice, because Samaritans were hated and despised by Jews, and woman were regarded as practically non-persons. To confound us even more, he adds, she is a woman whose married life is far from exemplary. But I want to ask: is it John the author or Jesus the Saviour who chooses the Samaritan woman? My vote is with the latter.

134 F.F. Bruce, *The Gospel of John*, 103, explains that the issue is not simply that Jews have no dealings with Samaritans, but rather that 'Jews and Samaritans ... do not share vessels in common'. This insight helps us to understand that in questioning the holy

stranger, the woman is challenging his understanding of his own Judaism – if she gave him a drink from her vessel, he would become ceremonially unclean.

135 There are various explanations of the symbolic meaning of the living water under discussion. See for example Carson, *John*, 217–19; Bruce, *Gospel*, 104; O'Day, *Revelation*, 60–3, L. Eslinger, 'The Wooing of the Woman at the Well: Jesus, the Reader and Reader-Response Criticism', *Journal of Literature and Theology* 1.2 (Sept. 1987), 170; Culpepper, *Anatomy*, 108; D.A. Lee, *The Symbolic Narratives of the Fourth Gospel – The Interplay of Form and Meaning*, 76–7; Talbert, *Reading John*, 113; Moore, *Deconstructive Criticism*, 54–60; Phillips, 'Ethics of Reading Deconstructively', 309. The meaning is fairly transparent, however: Jesus, the source of all life, is offering her eternal life, but the offer is dependent on the woman's acceptance and recognition of him.

136 P.D. Duke, *Irony in the Fourth Gospel*, 100, draws attention to the 'oft used device ... particularly of ancient dramatic irony ... of unknown or mistaken identity'.

137 Interestingly, Eslinger, 'Wooing of the Woman at the Well', 178, argues that the dialogue between Jesus and the woman is full of sexual innuendo and double entendre, and claims that 'Jesus tells her to get her husband exactly when she expected to commit adultery against the man.'

138 Whilst women did 'belong' to men, they were not treated as property in the same way as property or animals; but had a higher status, and were respected as individuals, even if, as today, they do not enjoy equal status.

139 Carson, *John*, 216, explains that the Assyrians, who captured Samaria in 722–721 BC deported Israelites of substance and settled the land with foreigners, who intermarried with the surviving Israelites and adhered to some form of their ancient religion. After the exile, when Jews returned to their homeland, the hatred between Jews and Samaritans was well established. Most of this history can be gleaned from the Bible (Genesis 24; 1 Kings 16:24; 2 Kings 17–18, Nehemiah 13), some from ancient historian Josephus.

140 O'Day, *Revelation*, 59, comments perceptively that 'Jesus does not answer in terms of Samaritan/Jewish relations, but in terms of his identity'.

141 Carson, *John*, 217, teaches that women were more likely to go in groups to fetch water, in the cool of the day, and that possibly,

because this women is at the well alone, she is ashamed of the lifestyle she is living (cf John 4:16), and that her isolated appearance is indicative of her loose morals. Schneiders, 'Women', 38, too, concedes to the woman's 'checkered past'. Talbert, *Reading John*, 112, drawing on historical studies in his literary analysis, uses ancient Jewish literature which advises against public conversation of a man with a woman, and which warns against Jewish contact with Samaritans drawing attention to the following: in which he cites 'He that talks much with womankind brings evil upon himself' (m. Pike Aboth 1:5) and 'It is forbidden to give a woman any greeting' (b. Kiddushim 70a), and, amongst others, 'The daughters of Samaria are deemed unclean as menstruants from their cradle' (M. Niddah 4:1). However, Maccini, 'Her Testimony', 40 argues that this 'Jewish precept cannot be projected automatically onto everyone in a story that takes place in Samaria.' He asserts that Pharisaic reckoning deemed some menstruates unclean at times when Samaritan reckoning did not and that even amongst Samaritans themselves codes regarding menstruates were not uniform. Also, 'Her Testimony', 135, Maccini argues that the Samaritans 'do not make any distinction between the sexes in reference to their common obligation to carry out the Law'. He further states, 'Because Samaritans interpreted the Pentateuch strictly, the injunction of Deuteronomy 31:12 indicates that their practice of educating children of both sexes in the law and Samaritan traditions is not an innovation but probably dates back to their origins', and argues that 'Samaritan dispositions toward women became increasingly sub-ordinationist only with time, particularly under Muslim influence'.

142 Carson, *John*, 232, (amongst others) notes allegorical interpretations where the five husbands are thought to represent five pagan deities, and the Samaritan woman represents the mixed and religiously tainted Samaritan race. The sixth man, to whom the woman was not legally married, represents either another false god, or more commonly, the true God to whom the Samaritans are connected only by an illicit union. Carson lays bare the error of this interpretation as the transported settlers worshipped seven pagan deities, not five – although there were five named cities – and these gods were all worshipped at the same time, not serially.

143 Mark 10:2 indicates that the issue of divorce was one on the contemporary theological agenda. Stott, *Issues*, 290, suggests

there were basically two schools of thought on the issue in Jesus' day – those who followed the teaching of Shammai who interpreted the 'something indecent' in Deuteronomy 24:1 as being a sexual offence, and those who followed Hillel, who claimed that 'becomes displeasing' could incorporate the most trivial action which caused irritation to the husband.

144 Carson, *John*, 216, is seriously in error when he asserts that the woman, in contrast to Nicodemus was 'unschooled, without influence, despised and capable only of folk religion'.

145 See Talbert, *Reading John* and Maccini, 'Her Testimony'; also Carson, *John*, 227 who states that providing daughters with a knowledge of the Torah was regarded as being as inappropriate as teaching them lechery.

146 Stibbe, *John's Gospel*, 67–8, argues that Jesus is now the seventh, and therefore perfect, man in her life: 'The woman of Samaria becomes the eschatological bride ... No longer is Israel alone the bride of Yahweh.'

147 Sadly for this hypothesis, there is no further mention of baptisms here. The writer of the Gospel may be preparing his audience for John 6, where Jesus feeds the five thousand (see especially John 6:5–6).

148 Eslinger, 'Wooing of the Woman at the Well'; Stibbe, *John's Gospel*; Lee, *Symbolic Narratives*; Culpepper, *Anatomy*.

Bibliography

Atkinson, David, *The Message of Ruth* (Leicester: IVP, 1983)

Bailey, Gordon, *Stuff and Nonsense: A Collection of Verse and Worse* (Oxford: Lion, 1989)

Barclay, William, *The Gospel of Matthew*, Vol. 1 (2 Vols.; Edinburgh: Saint Andrew Press, 1965)

Bauckham, Richard, 'The Beloved Disciple as Ideal Author', *JSNT* 49 (1993), 21–44

Beattie, D.R.B., 'Redemption in Ruth and Related Matters: A Response to Jack M. Sasson', *JSOT* 5 (1978), 65–8

—, 'Ruth III', *JSOT* 5 (1978), 39–48

Beeching, H.C. (ed.), *The Poetical Works of John Milton* (Oxford: Clarendon Press, 1900)

Benedikt, Michael (ed.), *Cyberspace: First Steps* (Cambridge, Mass./London: MIT Press, 1991)

Bernstein, Moshe, 'Two Multivalent Readings in the Ruth Narrative', *JSOT* 50 (1991), 15–26

Borrowdale, Anne, *A Woman's Work: Changing Christian Attitudes* (London: SPCK, 1989)

Brenner, Athalya (ed.), *A Feminist Companion to Ruth* (Sheffield: Sheffield Academic Press, 1993)

—, *The Israelite Woman: Social Role and Literary Type in Biblical Narrative* (Sheffield: JSOT Press, 1985)

Brestin, Dee, *The Friendships of Women* (Amersham-on-the-Hill: Scripture Press, 1994)

211

Brown, Raymond E., *The Gospel According to John, I-XII, Anchor Bible* (London: Geoffrey Chapman, 1966)

Browning, Robert, 'The Ring and the Book', VI. 2038, in *The Complete Poetical Works of Robert Browning* Vol. 8 (Athens, Ohio: Ohio University Press, 1988)

Bruce, F.F. *The Gospel of John* (London: Pickering and Inglis, 1983)

Campbell, E. Jr., 'Ruth' in *The Anchor Bible* (New York: Doubleday, 1975)

Carson, D.A. *The Gospel According to John* (Leicester: Inter-Varsity Press, 1991)

Cook, Robert, 'Postmodernism, Pluralism and John Hick', *Themelios* 19.1 (Oct 1993), 10–12

Coxon, Peter W., 'Was Naomi a Scold? A Response to Fewell and Gunn', *JSOT* 45 (1989), 25–37

Culpepper, R.A., *Anatomy of the Fourth Gospel: A Study in Literary Design* (Philadelphia: Fortress Press, 1983)

Davies, E.W., 'Inheritance Rights and the Hebrew Levirate Marriage, Part 1', *Vetus Testamentum* 31.2 (1981), 139–144

Davies, E.W., 'Inheritance Rights and the Hebrew Levirate Marriage, Part 2', *Vetus Testamentum* 31.3 (1981), 257–68

DeVaux, R., *Ancient Israel: Its Life and Institutions* (London: Darton, Longman & Todd, 1965)

Duke, Paul D., *Irony in the Fourth Gospel* (Atlanta: John Knox Press, 1985)

Eslinger, Lyle, 'The Wooing of the Woman at the Well: Jesus, the Reader and Reader-Response Criticism', *Journal of Literature and Theology* 1.2 (Sept. 1987), 167–83

Evans, Mary, *Woman in the Bible* (Exeter: Paternoster Press, 1983)

Fenton, John, *Finding the Way through John* (London: Mowbray, 1988)

Fewell, D.N. & D.M. Gunn, *Compromising Redemption: Relating Characters in the Book of Ruth* (Louisville: Westminster/John Knox Press, 1990)

—, 'Boaz, Pillar of Society: Measures of Worth in the Book of Ruth', *JSOT* 45 (1989), 45–59

—, 'Is Coxon a Scold? On Responding to the Book of Ruth', *JSOT* 45 (1989), 39–43

—, 'A Son is Born to Naomi!': Literary Allusions and Interpretation in the Book of Ruth', *JSOT* 40 (1988), 99–108

Fisch, Harold, 'Ruth and the Structure of Covenant History', *Vetus Testamentum* 32 (1982), 425–37

Freed, Edwin, D., 'Did John Write his Gospel Partly to Win Samaritan Converts?' *Novum Testamentum* 12 (1970), 241–56

Gellner, Ernest, *Postmodernism, Reason and Religion* (London: Routledge, 1992)

Gibson, William, *Neuromancer* (London: Grafton Books, 1989)

Grana, Janice, *Images: Women in Transition* (Nashville: The Upper Room, 1976)

Green, Barbara, 'The Plot of the Biblical Story of Ruth', *JSOT* 23 (1982), 55–68

Grenz, Stanley, 'Postmodernism and the Future of Evangelical Theology: Star Trek and the Next Generation', in *Evangelical Quarterly* (Oct. 1994), 322–34.

Hals, Ronald, M., *The Theology of Ruth* (Philadelphia: Fortress Press, 1969)

Harvey, David, *The Condition of Postmodernity* (Oxford: Blackwell, 1992)

Howard-Brook, Wes, *John's Gospel and the Renewal of the Church* (Maryknoll, NY: Orbis, 1997)

Hubbard Jr., Robert L., *The Book of Ruth* (NICOT; Grand Rapids: Eerdmans, 1988)

—, 'Ruth IV:17: A New Solution', *Vetus Testamentum* 38 (1988), 293–301

van Hyssteen, J. Wentzel, 'Is the Postmodernist Always a Postfoundationalist?', *Theology Today* October 1993, 373–86

Inbody, Tyron, 'Postmodernism – Intellectual Velcro Dragged Across Culture?', *Theology Today* (Jan. 1995), 524–38

Ingleby, J., Two Cheers for Postmodernism', in *Third Way*, May 1992, 24–7

Knight, G.A.F., *Ruth & Jonah: The Gospel in the Old Testament* (London: SCM Press, 1966)

Kroeger, Catherine C. & Mary J. Evans (eds.), *The IVP Women's Bible Commentary* (Leicester: Inter-Varsity Press, 2002)

Kübler-Ross, Elisabeth, *On Death and Dying* (London/New York: Tavistock Publications, 1969)

Laffey, Alice, L. *An Introduction to the Old Testament: A Feminist Perspective* (Philadelphia: Fortress Press, 1988)

Lawrence, D.H., 'Today', in Vivian de Sola Pinto and Warren Roberts (eds.), *The Complete Poems of D.H. Lawrence* Vol. 2 (London: William Heinemann, 1967)

Lee, Dorothy A., *The Symbolic Narratives of the Fourth Gospel – The Interplay of Form and Meaning* (*JSNT* Supplement Series 95, 1994)

Lyon, David, *Postmodernity* (Buckingham: Open University Press, 1994)

Maccini, Robert Gordon, *Her Testimony is True: Women as Witness According to John* (*JSNT*, Supplement Series 125, 1996)

Malcolm, Keri Torjesen, *Women at the Crossroads* (Leicester: Inter-Varsity Press, 1982)

McKnight, Edgar, V., *Post-Modern Use of the Bible: The Emergence of Reader-Oriented Criticism* (Nashville: Abingdon Press, 1988)

McQuilken, R & Mullen, B 'The Impact of Postmodern Thinking on Evangelical Hermeneutics', *JETS* 40.1 (Mar. 1997), 69–82

Mercer, Nick, 'Postmodernity and Rationality: The Final Credits or Just a Commercial Break?', in Antony Billington, Tony Lane & Max Turner (eds.), *Mission and Meaning: Essays Presented to Peter Cotterell* (Carlisle: Paternoster, 1995)

Morris, Leon, 'Ruth: Introduction and Commentary' in *Judges & Ruth* (London: Tyndale Press, 1968)

Neuhaus, Richard, 'A Voice in the Relativistic Wilderness' in *Christianity Today*, 7 February 1994

O'Day, Gail, *Revelation in the Fourth Gospel: Narrative Mode and Theological Claim* (Philadelphia: Fortress Press, 1986)

Patte, Daniel M., *Ethics of Biblical Interpretation: A Re-evaluation* (Louisville: Westminster John Knox Press, 1995)

Phillips, Gary A., 'The Ethics of Reading Deconstructively, or Speaking Face-to-Face: The Samaritan Woman Meets Derrida at the Well', in E.S. Malbon and E.V. McKnight (eds.), *The New Literary Criticism and the New Testament* (JSNT Supplement; Sheffield: Sheffield Academic Press, 1994), 283–325

Ramazanoglu, Caroline, 'Gender', *Sociology* 7.6 (1990), 137–57

Roseneil, Sasha, 'Gender', in *Sociology* 11.5 (1995), 87–103

Ruether, R. Radford, *Sexism and God-Talk: Toward a Feminist Theology* (London: SCM, 1983)

—, *Sexism and God-Talk* (London: SCM Press Ltd., 1983)

Sampson, P., V. Samuel & C. Sugden (eds.), *Faith and Modernity* (Oxford: Regnum, 1994)

Sasson, Jack M., *Ruth: A New Translation with a Philological Commentary and a Formalist-Folklorist Interpretation* (JSOT; Sheffield: Sheffield Academic Press, 1989)

—, 'Ruth III: A Response', *JSOT* 5 (1978), 52–64

—, 'The Issue of *Ge'ullah* in Ruth', *JSOT* 5 (1978), 52–64

Schneiders, Sandra, M., 'Women in the Fourth Gospel and the Role of Women in the Contemporary Church', *Biblical Theology Bulletin* 12.2 (April 1982), 35–44

Schüssler Fiorenza, Elisabeth, *Bread not Stone: The Challenge of Feminist Biblical Interpretation* (Edinburgh: T. & T. Clark, 1990)

Scraton, S. & P. Branham, 'Leisure & Postmodernity', *Sociology* 11 (1995), 98–108

Simmons, Gary & Tony Walter, 'Spot the Men: The relation of faith and gender', *Third Way*, 10 April 1988, 10–12

Smail, Thomas, A., *The Giving Gift: The Holy Spirit in Person* (London: Hodder and Stoughton, 1988)

Smith, Christine, M., 'Sin and Evil in Feminist Thought', *Theology Today*, July 1993, 208–19

Smith, David, 'The Premodern and the Postmodern: Some Parallels, with Special Reference to Hinduism', in *Religion* 23 (1993), 157–65

Stevie Smith, *Selected Poems* (ed. James McGibbon; London: Penguin, 1978)

Stibbe, Mark, W.G., *John's Gospel* (London: Routledge, 1994)

Storkey, Elaine, 'At the End of the Second Millennium – Where are all the Women?' (Henry Martyn Lecture, 1994; Evangelical Missionary Alliance)

—, *What's Right with Feminism?* (London: SPCK, 1985)

Stott, John, *Issues Facing Christians Today* (London: Marshall Pickering, 1990)

Talbert, Charles H., *Reading John: A Literary and Theological Commentary on the Fourth Gospel and the Johannine Epistles* (London: SPCK, 1992)

Tapia, Andres, 'Reaching the First Post-Christian Generation' in *Christianity Today*, 12 September 1994, 18–23

Tennyson, Alfred Lord, 'In Memoriam A.H.H.', in *The Complete Works of Alfred Lord Tennyson* (London: Macmillan, 1898)

Tester, Keith, 'Postmodernism', *Sociology* 11.7 (1995), 129–46

Thistlethwaite, Susan, *Sex, Race & God* (London: Geoffrey Chapman, 1990)

Tomlinson, Dave, *Post-Evangelicalism* (London: Triangle, 1995)

Trible, Phyllis, *God and the Rhetoric of Sexuality* (Philadelphia: Fortress Press, 1992 [1978])

Veith, Gene Edward, *Guide to Contemporary Culture* (Wheaton: Crossway Books, 1994)

Wallace, Ronald S. *The Gospel of John, Chapters 1-11 Pastoral and Theological Studies including some sermons* (Edinburgh: Scottish Academic Press, 1991)

Walters, Tony, 'Why are most churchgoers women?', *Vox Evangelica* (1980), 73–90

Wilson, Robert, R., *Sociological Approaches to the Old Testament* (Philadelphia: Fortress Press, 1984)

Witherington, Ben, *Women and the Genesis of Christianity* (Cambridge: Cambridge University Press, 1990)

Yancey, Philip, 'The Lost Sex Study', *Christianity Today* 12 December 1994, 80